Sean O'Byrne

ESSENTIALS

GCSE ICT

Information & Communication Technology

Revision Guide

Contents

Contents

Modern Living

Computer Systems

What is a Computer?

A computer is an electronic machine that processes data. It follows **instructions** given to it in the form of a **program**.

Computers are everywhere these days and there are many different types.

Personal Computers (PCs)

Most people are familiar with **general purpose computers**. These computers can run a wide variety of programs, which make them do different things, for example, word processing or creating electricity bills.

The PC (**personal computer**) is a general purpose computer. It comes in various forms, e.g. a desktop PC, a laptop, a PDA or even a mobile phone.

Laptops	Personal Digital Assistants (PDAs) or Palm Tops	Mobile Phones
Many people work on the move these days and use portable computers. Some laptops are small and light, whilst others have large screens that are useful for work or watching films.	A PDA is a small, hand-held computer that can be used… <ul><li>as a PC</li><li>for web browsing</li><li>as a mobile phone</li><li>as a portable media player.</li></ul> Some PDAs have a touch screen and are controlled using a **stylus**. 	Mobile phones are the most commonly used computers in the world. They have a processor and memory and can run programs.
Netbooks have built in **WiFi** access, **webcams**, speakers and microphones. They are very small and light. They save weight by not having a CD or DVD drive or, in some cases, a hard drive. But, netbooks can be fiddly to use because of their small keys and screens.		**WAP** stands for **Wireless Access Protocol**. This is a set of **standards** that allows PDAs and mobile phones to access the Internet.
The latest portable computers have enough battery life to allow someone to work most of the day on one charge.		Some computers have become more like mobile phones, whilst some mobile phones have become more like general purpose computers. A **smart phone** is a device that's mainly concerned with phone functions but also has email, Internet and other features.

Mainframe Computers

Mainframe computers are large, expensive computers that can support many users at the same time. Big organisations use mainframes to run their most important jobs. The term **mini computer** is used to refer to smaller mainframes.

Supercomputers are the fastest of all computers. They're needed where vast numbers of calculations are carried out, for example, in weather forecasting. Supercomputers run a few programs very fast rather than running lots of programs at the same time.

Mainframe Computers

Computer Systems

A **system** is a collection of parts that work together for a particular purpose, for example, the human digestive system. We use systems in everyday life, such as transport and banking systems.

A computer system is a collection of items working together and controlled by a computer. Mobile phones, microwaves and car engines are all controlled by computer systems.

Embedded Systems

Some computers are designed to work in just one particular situation. These are called **dedicated computers**.

Most modern electronic devices have computer systems inside them that control them. These are called **embedded systems**. Developing embedded systems is one of the fastest growing branches of computing.

Digital watch:
An example of a
device containing an
embedded system

Quick Test

1. What is a computer system?
2. Give one advantage and one disadvantage of using a Netbook when working on the move.
3. List three household items that are controlled by an embedded system.
4. What is a dedicated computer?

KEY WORDS
Make sure you understand these words before moving on!
- Instructions
- Program
- General purpose computer
- Personal computer
- WiFi
- Webcam
- Standards
- Smart phone
- System
- Dedicated computer
- Embedded system

Hardware

Hardware

The **hardware** of a computer system is all the equipment that you can see and touch. It includes the devices that you work with as well as all the components that are inside the box.

Central Processing Unit (CPU)

The **Central Processing Unit** (CPU) is known as the **processor** or the **microprocessor** (because it's so small). The CPU is a set of electronic circuits that control the computer by running the programs. The programs are stored in **RAM**.

The microprocessor is made from billions of transistors. The more there are, the faster the processor can work. The technology is still advancing and Moore's Law states that the number of transistors in processors doubles every two years.

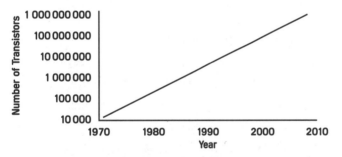

The **control unit** of the processor runs the programs and directs operations. The processor carries out calculations and comparisons in its **Arithmetic Logic Unit** (ALU).

The processor contains a clock that 'ticks' a certain number of times every second. The clock times when program instructions will be carried out. The more 'ticks' per second, the faster the computer. The clock speed is measured in multiples of Hertz, for example:

> Intel® Pentium® Dual-Core Processor E5300 (2.6GHz, 800FSB, 2MB cache)

This means that the clock speed is 2.6GHz (Gigahertz):
- 2.6 x 1024 x 1024 x 1024 = 2791728742.4 ticks per second.

Circuit Boards

Motherboards

All of the electronic components in a computer are attached to a plastic card called a **motherboard**. The connections are printed onto the board and the components are plugged in or soldered into position.

Sound Card

On some computers there's a special set of circuits that produce sound signals, which go to a loudspeaker. On most PCs, sound cards are integrated onto the motherboard.

Video Card

A video card is a set of circuits, which produce the electrical signals that make the image on the screen. Again, it's often integrated onto the motherboard. Some computers have separate high-quality video cards that are useful for playing games or displaying films.

> Video card: Integrated Intel Graphics Media Accelerator 3100

Memory

It's important to know how much memory a computer has. Memory comes in two types:

- **ROM**
- **RAM**

ROM stands for Read-Only Memory. Computers don't need much ROM because it just contains the basic instructions to get the computer started at boot up. The instructions are there all the time even when the computer is switched off.

RAM stands for Random Access Memory. RAM stores data and a computer needs a lot of RAM. This data is all stored in the same way – in groups of 1s and 0s. Each 1 or 0 is called a **bit** (Binary Digit) of data. RAM is usually divided up into groups of eight bits and, generally, eight bits make 1 **byte**.

For example:

> Memory: 3072MB 800MHz Dual Channel
> DDR2 SDRAM (3x1024)

This means that there are 3072MB (Megabytes) of RAM (this is the same as 3GB (Gigabytes)). That's over 3 billion bytes. Having a lot of RAM is useful when running several programs at the same time and adding more RAM can make a big difference to the speed of a computer.

The data in RAM can represent many things. For example, in different parts of RAM there may be at any time…

- data on its way to the processor
- data on its way from the processor
- data being worked on
- program instructions.

Data is often queued up in RAM whilst waiting to be processed. A part of RAM used for that purpose is called a **buffer**. For example, a printer buffer stores data that's waiting to be sent to a printer.

RAM isn't used for processing. Data is sent to the processor to be worked on, then the results are stored in RAM. RAM loses all of its data when the power is switched off.

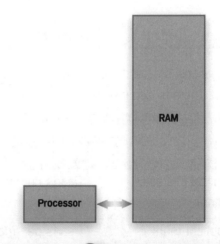

Quick Test

1. What type of memory loses its data when the computer is switched off?
2. Where are calculations carried out in a computer?
3. A computer is advertised as having 5GB of RAM. How many bytes is that?
4. What is the smallest unit of data called?

KEY WORDS

Make sure you understand these words before moving on!

- Processor
- RAM
- Control Unit
- Arithmetic Logic Unit
- ROM
- Bit
- Byte
- Buffer

Input Devices

Input Devices

Input devices are needed to put data into a computer. These devices normally convert physical energy into electrical pulses, which the computer can accept.

You should be able to work out what input devices are needed for a range of...

- processor-controlled devices
- common PC-based devices.

Webcam

The table shows some common input devices used with PCs.

Input Device	Comments
Keyboard	Used for inputting data into small computer systems
Mouse	Used to select and move objects on the screen
Touch pad	Alternative to mouse on laptops
Webcam and microphone	Useful for chatting and video conferencing
Scanners	For **digitising** images
Joystick / game controller	Used for interacting with games
Touch screen	Used for data input in public places, mobile phones, etc.

Automated Data Input

In organisations, time and money can be saved by automating data input. There is also less risk of mistakes if machines do the input. A few examples are given in the table below:

Input Device / Method	Comments	Uses
OCR (optical character recognition)	Reads human readable letters	• Number plate recognition, e.g. speed cameras
OMR (optical mark recognition)	Reads pen marks on pre-printed forms	• Multiple-choice exams • Lottery entries
MICR (magnetic ink character recognition)	Special ink that machines can read	• Cheque processing
Bar code scanner	Reads the bars on products	• Supermarket checkouts
Magnetic stripe reader	Reads a small amount of data on a card	• Used on the back of credit / debit cards • Train tickets and car park tickets
Smart card reader	Reads and writes data to a chip on a card	• Credit / debit cards (chip and pin) • Travel cards • Satellite viewer boxes
RFID	Radio frequency identification	• Travel cards (e.g. Oyster card) • Identifying products in shops

Sensors

Like other input devices, **sensors** detect events in the real world and produce electrical signals. Real-world energy is **analogue**, which means that it varies continuously. For example, the temperature of a room can be anything (within certain limits).

Computers need to read **digital** signals, which are either **on** or **off.** So, the output from sensors needs to be converted from analogue to digital signals, using an analogue to digital convertor, before it can be used by a computer.

Different types of sensors are shown in the table below:

Sensor	Example of Use
Heat	Computer controlled greenhouse
Light	Digital cameras
Pressure	Burglar alarms
Electrical inductance	Traffic lights
pH	Chemical manufacturing processes

Use of Sensors

Sensors can be used for collecting data in many situations. They are often linked to output in order to automate systems.

You need to be able to recognise what sensors may be used in a given situation.

For example:
- Touch sensitive buttons in a lift.
- Oxygen levels in a car exhaust.
- Tyre temperatures in a racing car.
- Vibration sensors to detect earthquakes.
- Air pressure in an aircraft altimeter.

Quick Test

1. What type of signals can computers recognise?
2. Give one reason why businesses try to automate data input.
3. Give one use for OMR data input.
4. Give one input device used in a bank cash machine (ATM).

KEY WORDS

Make sure you understand these words before moving on!
- Input devices
- Digitising
- OCR
- OMR
- Bar code
- RFID
- Sensor
- Analogue
- Digital

Output Devices

Output Devices

Computers exist to produce **output**, which can be in many forms.

When designing a computer system, an important design skill is to understand how the output will be presented.

Computers process the data they are given as **input**. They then pass back the results as **output.** The output might be passed to a human or to another device or piece of machinery.

Printed output is called **hard copy.** Hard copy can be used…

* to look at when there isn't access to a computer
* as proof that something took place.

Common Output Devices with PCs

PCs are normally used to produce visual or sound output for humans. But, they are increasingly used as communication devices as well as data processing devices.

Output Device	Comments
Screen / VDU (visual display unit)	• Most are now thin film transistor liquid crystal display (**TFT-LCD**). • Older ones are Cathode Ray Tubes (CRT) but these run hot and take up more space.
Laser printer	• High quality fast output. • Uses powdered **toner** to make the image.
Ink jet printer	• High quality – good for home colour use. • Quite slow and the ink is very expensive.
Dot matrix printer	• Cheap, noisy, poor quality but useful on multi-part stationery. • Often seen in garages and builders' yards to produce invoices.
Thermal printer	• Used for printing supermarket receipts.
Speakers	• Used for playing music, films or chatting. • If used with a microphone, they can produce noisy feedback effects.
Headphones	• Better quality sound for chatting. • No feedback.
Digital projector	• Used for displaying computer output to an audience.
Touch screen	• Output as well as input device. • Can give an easy-to-use menu, (e.g. on railway ticket machines).

Specialist Output Devices

There is a huge range of output devices that are designed for a particular purpose.

For example:

- **Plotter** – used for large drawings and plans, e.g. architects' designs. The computer guides a pen over the paper.
- **Actuators** – devices that switch circuits on and off, e.g. opening a valve in an industrial process.
- **Lights** – controlled by computer output, e.g. stage lights in a theatre or traffic lights.
- **Motors** – many uses, e.g. an aircraft's autopilot controlling the wing flaps.
- **Robot arms** – used in manufacturing.

Output Devices in the Home

There are many electronic devices in the home. They all have their own output.

A microwave oven has a…
- motor for turning the turntable
- magnetron for producing the microwaves
- speaker to alert the user to the end of the program.

A washing machine has a…
- motor to turn the drum
- panel to show the state of the cycle
- heater to warm the water.

A DVD player has output signals that are sent to the TV screen for display. It has a…
- display panel to show details of what is playing, the time, etc.
- motor to spin the DVD.

Quick Test

1. Give one reason why a customer would want a bill produced in hard copy.
2. Give one advantage of a TFT-LCD over a CRT screen.
3. What type of printer is used for printing on multi-part stationery?
4. What professions might make use of a plotter?

KEY WORDS

Make sure you understand these words before moving on!

- Output
- Input
- Hard copy
- TFT-LCD
- Toner
- Plotter
- Actuator

Storage Devices

Memory

The smallest unit of memory is 1 **bit**. A bit can **only** be 0 or 1. Most modern computers organise data into **bytes** consisting of 8 bits.

Numbers

1 Byte:

Place Value	128	64	32	16	8	4	2	1
Bit Value	0	1	0	0	0	0	0	1

Each place value in a **byte** is worth twice as much as the place to its right. In the byte above, we have a 1 in the 64 place and a 1 in the 1 place. That means that the number stored is 64 + 1 = 65. This number can also be used as a code for different things.

Characters

The **ASCII** code (American Standard Code for Information Interchange) uses a number to represent each character or letter. For example, 65 represents the capital letter 'A'. Another system, called **Unicode**, allows the storage of characters from all languages.

Pictures

Bytes can be used to store a set of dots of different colours (**pixels**). These pixels can be mapped to a screen display or a printer. This is called a bit-mapped image and it can take over a million bytes to store an image.

Music

Sounds can be sampled for pitch, loudness and other qualities. The samples can be stored as numbers. The more numbers that are collected, the better the quality of the sound. Digital sound can be played back on a digital device, e.g. an **MP3 player**.

Instructions

The **instructions** in a computer program are also stored as bytes. All stored data is in the same form. The computer knows what to do with the data according to the program instructions and where the data is stored.

1 byte is enough data to code for 1 character. Modern computers store vast amounts of data, so we use other units to measure groups of bytes.

Unit	Meaning
Kilobyte (KB)	1024 bytes
Megabyte (MB)	1024 KB
Gigabyte (GB)	1024 MB
Terabyte (TB)	1024 GB

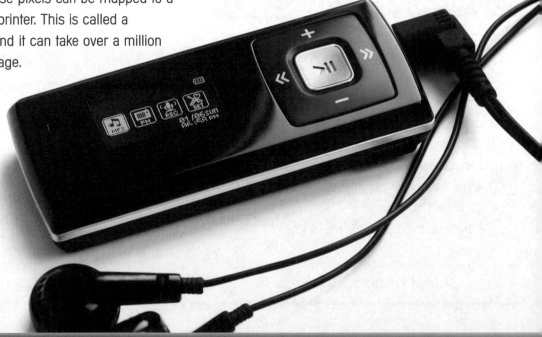

Primary Storage

There are two types of primary storage:

- **RAM**
- **ROM**

RAM

RAM (Random Access Memory) stores the data and instructions that are currently being used. Data must be in RAM before it can be processed. RAM loses its contents when the power is switched off.

Cache Memory

Cache memory is a small store of fast memory that copies data from the most frequently accessed parts of main memory. The processor checks the cache first to see if the data or instruction it needs next is there. If it is, it saves the time it would take to access the slower main RAM.

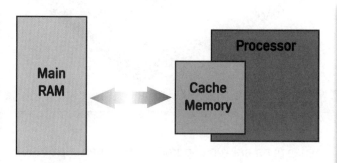

ROM

The data in **ROM** (Read-Only Memory) can be accessed by the processor, but it can't put new data into it.

ROM keeps its data when the computer is switched off. It stores the basic instructions to allow the computer to boot up, i.e. load the operating system software. ROM is used to store programs in embedded systems such as mobile phones, washing machines and MP3 players.

Flash memory is a type of ROM that can be erased and reprogrammed thousands of times. It's used in secondary storage. Embedded systems increasingly use flash memory because it can be updated.

PC RAM Memory

Quick Test

1. What is the smallest unit of data that a computer can process?
2. How much memory is normally used to store one letter?
3. What are the dots called that make up a picture when stored in a computer?
4. What type of memory loses its data when the power is switched off?

KEY WORDS

Make sure you understand these words before moving on!

- Bit
- Byte
- ASCII
- Unicode
- Pixels
- MP3 player
- Instructions
- Kilobyte
- Megabyte
- Gigabyte
- Terabyte
- RAM
- ROM
- Flash memory

Secondary Storage

Reasons for Secondary Storage

Secondary storage is used to hold data for the future. It's sometimes called **backing storage** and has become faster and cheaper in recent years.

Secondary storage is also useful for taking additional copies of important data in case of problems. This is called **backing up**.

Flash Memory

USB Drive

A **USB drive**, also known as a memory stick or a pen drive, connects to the computer via a USB port. We normally store lots of data on USB drives, and it's an example of flash memory.

Advantages:
- Small and easily transportable
- Very large capacity
- Can be written to and erased over a million times
- No moving parts

Disadvantages:
- Easily lost – there have been cases where lots of sensitive data has gone missing on USB drives.

Memory Cards

Memory cards are flash memory devices designed to fit into cameras, MP3 players and mobile computers. Modern computers normally come with a memory card slot so that data can be transferred to the computer.

Virtual Memory

When a big program is running, it can be split into parts to fit into the available memory. Some parts can be temporarily stored on the hard disk while other parts are running from RAM. When a part is needed, it is 'swapped' back into RAM. The hard disk is being used as **virtual memory** (i.e. not real memory).

Optical Storage

Different types of optical storage vary according to what they can do. They all use lasers or other light to make and read patterns on a disk.

Examples:
- **Read-only: CD-ROM, DVD-ROM**
- **Read-write:** CD-R (Recordable), CD-RW (Re-Writable), DVD-RAM, DVD-R, DVD-RW
- **Blu-ray:** This is a standard that allows more data to be stored on an optical disk. It uses a shorter wavelength laser than CDs and DVDs.

Secondary Storage

Magnetic Storage

Hard Disks

Hard disks have very large capacity storage, based on magnetic technology.

Advantages:
- The most cost-effective way to provide a lot of storage on a PC system
- Fast data storage and retrieval
- Random access

Disadvantages:
- Can be damaged by knocks
- May need to be defragmented from time to time
- Adds weight to portable PCs

Some new PC systems are replacing hard disks with large-scale flash memory. The cost of flash memory is likely to come down, making this more attractive.

Magnetic Cartridges

Magnetic cartridges are tape based, and use magnetic technology just as hard disks do. They are commonly used to back up large amounts of data in network operations.

Advantages:
- Cheap high-capacity storage

Disadvantages:
- Slow data transfer
- Only supports sequential access. This means that the tape drive can't jump straight to the data required; it has to read in all the earlier data first.

Online Storage

Some businesses store their data online. Services such as Google Docs™ provide software and storage. 'Software As a Service' is an idea where you don't buy a licence, you just load software from the Internet.

Individuals often store photographs online so that their friends can see them too.

Advantages:
- No need to upgrade software
- No need to maintain storage infrastructure
- Easy to share resources
- Only need a web browser

Disadvantages:
- Loss of control over data storage
- May lose access to data if provider has a problem
- Can only access data when online

Quick Test

1. Give one disadvantage of backing data up on a USB drive (memory stick).
2. What type of light is used to read a CD-ROM disk?
3. What technology is used to store data on a hard disk?
4. When virtual memory is used, what part of a computer is used to add more memory to that in RAM?

KEY WORDS
Make sure you understand these words before moving on!
- Secondary storage
- USB drive
- Memory cards
- Virtual memory
- Read-only
- CD-ROM
- DVD-ROM
- Hard disk

Portable Computing

Battery Life

Sometimes working on the move can be restricted if the battery loses its power. This is more likely when using wireless connections, but the latest lithium-ion batteries together with power management systems can now support long working periods.

Range of Portable Devices

Computing devices can now be made in such small sizes that they are capable of being easily carried around. This has allowed the invention of many new portable products.

The number of features packed into these small devices has also increased.

Mobile Phones (Cell Phones)

Most phones are now much more than just phones. They typically have…
- still cameras (with high resolution)
- video recorders
- **MP3** players
- large amounts of memory
- the ability to add memory cards
- email connectivity
- the ability to connect to other networks and devices with **WiFi** and **Bluetooth**
- Internet connectivity with WAP (wireless application protocol).

Benefits:
- Can communicate from more or less anywhere
- Many functions in one device
- Can record events (useful for news items or crime scenes)

Problems:
- Small key sizes
- Easily tracked (invasion of privacy)
- Must be within range of a base station – inaccessible from some locations, e.g. in train tunnels or in mountainous areas

Personal Computers

Lightweight computers, such as netbooks, laptops and notebooks make working and communicating on the move easy. They are often full-featured PCs with WiFi, Bluetooth, USB ports, card readers, webcam, microphone and speakers.

Some keep costs and size down by…
- eliminating the hard disk and CD/DVD drive (it is replaced with solid state flash memory)
- providing an **Open Source** system and application software
- having a small screen.

Benefits:
- Ultra portable and can be used anywhere

Problems:
- Small key sizes
- Can be easily lost or stolen

Media Players

Media players combine several technologies to make a useful product. For example:
- Flash memory
- File compression standards
  - **sound:** MP3, Windows Media Audio
  - **video:** MPEG-4, Windows Media Video (WMV)

But, media have to be compressed to fit in the available memory. This can affect playback quality.

Cameras and Camcorders

The quality of digital still and film cameras improves all the time. The resolution is measured in **megapixels** (millions of dots). The more megapixels there are the better the image quality, but more storage is needed.

Range of Portable Devices (Cont.)

Navigation Aids

Portable navigation aids (sat navs) use computing devices to communicate with satellites to determine their location on the Earth's surface. This is called a Global Positioning System (**GPS**). By receiving signals from at least three satellites (triangulation), the location can be pinpointed to an accuracy of a few metres. In reality, normally 4 satellites are used.

The position is fed into a map database so that a display and / or audio commentary can be produced.

Connectivity Technologies

When using a mobile computer, there are choices to be made in order to stay connected, and making the right choice can make a big difference.

You have to choose the right hardware and service provider as well as use the correct **protocols.** Protocols are the rules and standards that devices use when communicating with each other.

Bluetooth

Bluetooth is a wireless protocol used for communicating over short distances.

Many different devices can be connected with Bluetooth, e.g. mobile phones, laptops and other PCs, printers, GPS systems, digital cameras and video game consoles.

Bluetooth can be used for distances up to 100 metres.

The following are some uses of Bluetooth:
* Setting up a personal network of different devices.
* Being able to print invoices in customers' homes by connecting to a portable printer with Bluetooth (useful for gas fitters, electricians, etc).
* A hands-free ear piece that can connect to a mobile phone.

WiFi

WiFi (short for Wireless Fidelity) is a way for computers to connect to a network. It's based on a standard known as **IEEE 802.11**. This is a set of rules that ensures that connected devices work together.

Most new PCs come with a WiFi adapter so that they can connect to a WiFi access point, **hotspot** or **router.** This usually gives onward access to the Internet.

Hotspots are common in many cafés, hotels and airports. Some cities have set up networks of hotspots to encourage visitors, and many hotels provide access for free.

WiFi is becoming an essential part of travelling both for business and pleasure. Delegates at meetings and conferences expect to be able to get online at any time.

Many people have wireless routers in the home. WiFi-enabled gadgets in the home can be controlled when you are away.

But, WiFi has a limited **range**. To work well, the computer needs to be no more than 30 metres from the hotspot, or 100 metres outdoors.

Portable Computing

Mobile Broadband

Mobile phone providers allow laptop access to the Internet via a **dongle.** This is a device that plugs into the USB port, contains a SIM card and works through the mobile phone network.

It sends signals to the nearest base station which connects to the telephone system.

Tomislav Stajduhar / Thinkstock

Advantages:
- Extends the range of places where Internet access is possible.
- Doesn't need to use WiFi providers (which can be very expensive).
- Connection speeds of 1Mbps (Mb/sec) are sometimes possible (usually in cities where there's good mobile phone coverage).

Disadvantages:
- The signal from the base station is often weak.
- The **bandwidth** can be much less than the maximum advertised. This can make connection speeds so slow that they are unusable.
- There are some connection issues, e.g. connection is lost when in tunnels and basements.
- There may be extra charges if you download too much data.

Bandwidth

Bandwidth literally means the range of frequencies carried in a communication link. But it has also come to mean the rate at which data is delivered. The rate is measured in bits per second (**bps**).

Bigger units are kilobits per second (**kbps**) and megabits per second (**mbps**):
- 1 kbps is 1000 bps.
- 1 mbps is 1 000 000 bps.

Note that unlike with data storage, multiples of 1024 are not generally used.

Broadband

Broadband refers to a communication link that delivers data at 256 kbps or more. You need at least this rate to make a connection usable. You need even more when transferring a lot of data, e.g. films or music files.

Protocols

The following are some common protocols used for personal communications:
- **TCP/IP (Transmission Control Protocol / Internet Protocol)** – the set of protocols that are used to control communications on the Internet and other networks.
- **VoIP (Voice Over Internet Protocol)** – allows telephone calls to be made using services such as Skype™.
- **POP (Post Office Protocol)** – allows retrieval of email from a TCP/IP server.

- **IMAP (Internet Message Access Protocol)** – another email retrieval set of standards as is SMTP (Simple Mail Transfer Protocol).
- **HTTP (Hypertext Transfer Protocol)** – controls the sending of web pages. HTTPS adds the word *secure*, which means that a page is **encrypted**. This is useful for sending bank details or credit card numbers.

Problems with Portable Computing

One of the main problems with portable computing is the issue of **security.**

It's easy to intercept wireless signals, so various methods have to be used to ensure privacy:

* Signals can be encrypted (i.e. scrambled) so that only authorised people have the key to decode them.
* The access point can be set up with **WEP** (Wireless Equivalent Privacy). This uses a 40-bit key to scramble the signals. Without this key it's not possible to gain access to the hotspot.
* **WPA2** (WiFi Protected Access) is a more secure method of connecting to a hotspot.
* **SSID** (Service Set Identifier) is a name for the network that's accessed via the hotspot. This can be hidden to lower the risk of it being used by unauthorised people.
* **MAC address** (Media Access Control) is a unique number assigned to each network card. The access point can be set to allow only certain MAC addresses to have access.

Other problems include the following:

* **Volume problems** – if lots of users try to access one connection point at the same time, the available bandwidth is divided between them. This leads to a lower performance.
* **Power consumption** – the battery life of a device is shortened when using wireless communication.

Quick Test

1. Give one reason why a mobile phone signal might not be available.
2. Name one file format used to store compressed sound files.
3. What is the smallest number of satellites needed to pinpoint the location of a GPS sat nav device?
4. What is the name of the set of rules used to connect devices for communication?
5. What is a connection that delivers data at a fast rate called?
6. What is a MAC address?

KEY WORDS
Make sure you understand these words before moving on!

* MP3
* WiFi
* Bluetooth
* Open Source
* GPS
* Protocol
* Bandwidth
* bps
* kbps
* mbps
* TCP/IP
* VoIP
* WEP

* IEEE 802.11
* Hotspot
* Router
* WPA2
* SSID
* MAC address

Networks

Why Network?

A network is a group of connected computers and other devices. Each device is called a **node**.

Most personal computers are connected to a network for at least some of the time.

The Internet is the biggest network of all. It's made up of lots of connected networks.

Benefits of Networks

There are many advantages to a computer network:

- Networked computers can all use the same printer and other peripherals.
- Computers can use the same data, which allows lots of people to work on a project at the same time.
- Users can communicate on the network and they can log in anywhere and on any machine.
- The processing power of many computers can be combined. This is called **distributed processing**.
- The computers can load software from the same location, which means the users will all have the same version of software. This makes it easier to upgrade the software because only one copy needs to be replaced.

Drawbacks of Networks

There are also drawbacks to networks:

- Networks can be expensive to set up and maintain.
- They may need specialist staff to look after them.
- There needs to be good security to keep data safe. The use of login credentials and access rights are essential.

Your user login ID connects you to a network, and if your password is correct you will be assigned certain access rights and privileges. This means that you have all the resources you need but can't access or damage data that doesn't concern you.

Internal and External Networks

Most organisations run their own networks. This lets them have total control over the safety of their data, but it also means that they have to take the risks that go with running their own networks.

Some organisations outsource their networking. They may set up a **VPN** (Virtual Private Network). This is held on a remote server and is accessed from any Internet-connected computer. Connections have to be encrypted because the data travels over public links.

Components

A **NIC** (**Network Interface Card**) is needed for each device so that it can send and receive the network signals.

Carrier Medium

Devices need to be connected via a **carrier medium.**

Medium	Advantages	Disadvantages
Metal cable	• Uses electrical signals. • Cheap to buy.	• Limited capacity may cause problems in installation.
Fibre optic cable	• Uses light beams. • High capacity, resistant to interference and weathering.	• Expensive. • Needs special NICs.
Wireless	• No need for building work. • Easy to add new nodes.	• Security is more difficult to achieve. • Limited range.

Hubs and Switches

Hubs and **switches** are devices that connect lots of computers to the carrier medium:
- **Hubs** are passive – they send data to all connections.
- **Switches** can send data in specific directions.

Wiring Cabinet

Wireless Router

Noraznen Azit / Thinkstock

Quick Test

1. What hardware is needed in each computer to connect to a network?
2. State one advantage in using wireless technology to set up a network.
3. What two items of data do you need to log in to a network?
4. Name a device that connects many computers to one carrier line.

KEY WORDS
Make sure you understand these words before moving on!
- Node
- Distributed processing
- VPN
- NIC
- Carrier medium
- Fibre optic
- Hub
- Switch

Types of Network

LAN and WAN

A **LAN** (**Local Area Network**) is a network on one site. The connecting hardware is owned by the same organisation that owns the network. LANs allow an organisation to have complete control over its data.

A **WAN** (**Wide Area Network**) covers a large geographical area, possibly even the whole world. The Internet is the biggest WAN. The connections will include hardware and services provided by another company, e.g. telecoms companies. In some cases, the company uses a **leased line** where it pays for exclusive use of connections.

Client-server

A **client-server** is where one or more computers act as a service provider to others. The services often include security, printing and file storage. The provider is a powerful computer called a **server**. The other computers are called **clients.** Some client-server networks have hundreds of servers.

Peer-to-Peer (P2P)

In a **peer-to-peer** system, all computers are equal. It's only suitable for very small networks, although the idea is used on the Internet to allow file sharing without the need to go through a server.

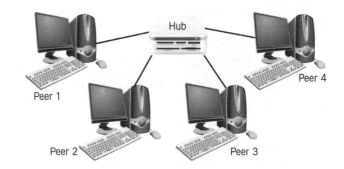

Topology

Topology is the way that a LAN is laid out. A LAN may be laid out as a bus, star or ring network. Most LANs in large organisations are now set out as **star** networks.

- It's slow when busy because of data collisions.
- Terminators are needed to prevent signals from being reflected.

Bus

In a **bus** network, all the computers are attached to a cable backbone.

Advantages:
- Simple and cheap to set up.

Disadvantages:
- Limited length.
- If the cable is disrupted, the whole network goes down.

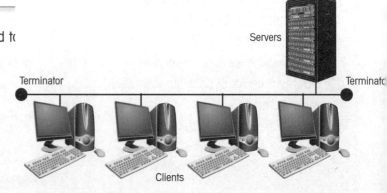

Star

In a **star** network, the client machines are connected to a central switch that attaches them to whichever servers are required.

Advantages:
- Easy to add extra clients.
- Fewer data collisions.
- No disruption to the rest of the network if one connection fails.

Disadvantages:
- Can be expensive to set up (building work may be required).

Ring

In a **ring** network, a common cable passes through each machine. The data passes round in one direction.

Advantages:
- Few collisions so it runs fast.

Disadvantages:
- If the cable is disrupted, the whole network goes down.

Star Network

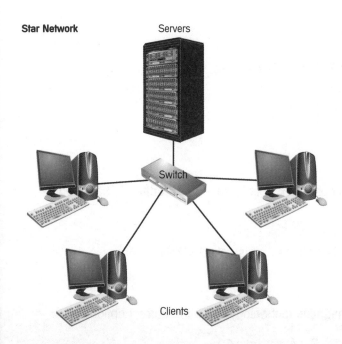

Servers

Switch

Clients

Ring Network

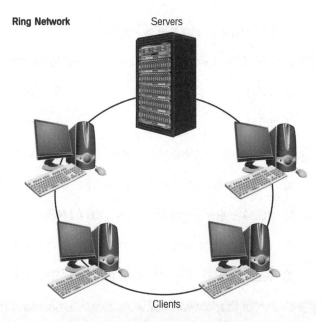

Servers

Clients

Quick Test

1. What is a network called if it's confined to one site?
2. What is a server?
3. What happens if the cable on a bus network is broken?
4. In what type of network are all the computers of equal status?

KEY WORDS

Make sure you understand these words before moving on!
- LAN
- WAN
- Leased line
- Client-server
- Server
- Peer-to-peer
- Topology
- Star
- Bus
- Ring

Practice Questions

1 Which of the following devices is the smallest? Tick the correct option.

A A laptop ◯ **B** A desktop ◯

C A notebook ◯ **D** A PDA ◯

2 What is the name of a computer system that is part of another device? Tick the correct option.

A An embedded system ◯ **B** An information system ◯

C An operating system ◯ **D** A real time system ◯

3 Fill in the missing words to complete the following sentences.

ASCII code is used by computers to store .... An alternative system is more flexible and

it's called .... Pictures are stored as a series of dots called ....

and this type of storage is known as a .... file.

4 Which of the following are file compression formats? Tick the **two** correct options.

A MP3 ◯ **B** JPG ◯ **C** DOC ◯

D HTM ◯ **E** BMP ◯ **F** XML ◯

5 (Circle) the correct options in the following sentences.

a) A network connection that delivers data at 256kbps or more is known as **broadband / baseband**.

b) 1024 bytes is the same as **1KB / 1MB**.

c) Memory that keeps its contents after the power is switched off is called **ROM / RAM**.

d) IEEE 802.11 is a standard for **WiFi / Bluetooth**.

6 Which of the following devices stores data using magnetic technology? Tick the correct option.

A A memory stick ◯ **B** A hard disk ◯

C A CD-ROM ◯ **D** RAM ◯

7 Choose the correct words from the options given to complete the following sentences.

| **SSID** | **hotspot** | **WEP** | **WPA2** | **encrypted** |

When connecting to a wireless ...., it's important that your signals are

.... so that if anyone intercepts them, they will not be able to understand them. If you use

.... to do this, using a 40-bit key, you will usually be safe, but ....

is even more secure. You should also hide your .... so that nobody can see your network.

8 Select the correct words from the list to complete the following sentences.

> **database**   **sat nav**   **3**   **speech synthesiser**   **triangulation**   **software**

A .... is a device that people have in their cars to allow them to know exactly

where they are. It receives data from at least .... satellites so that it can calculate

its position using a process called .... It feeds this result into a

.... which is stored in the system and uses .... to display

this on a map. The system often uses a .... to give audible directions to the driver.

9 Fill in the missing words to complete the following sentences.

A PC is switched on. As it boots up, its .... is copied

from the .... into .... , from where

it can be run. Each instruction is copied to the .... , where it is carried out.

10 Which of the following are protocols concerned with accessing email? Tick the **two** correct options.

A VoIP ⬡   **B** POP ⬡   **C** WAP ⬡

D IMAP ⬡   **E** IP ⬡   **F** HTTP ⬡

11 Match statements **A–E** to the correct type of network **1–5** in the table. Enter the appropriate numbers in the boxes provided.

1	LAN	**2**	Client-server	**3**	Bus	**4**	Star	**5**	Peer-to-peer

A All the computers in this network are of equal status ⬡

B The services are all stored on a central powerful computer ⬡

C If one cable is disconnected, the rest of the network carries on as normal ⬡

D The end of the cable has a terminator connected to it ⬡

E All the network components are located at one site ⬡

12 Explain why you need a lot of bandwidth in order to download music files from the Internet.

....

....

Software

Software

Software refers to the programs that a computer runs. A computer without software would be useless.

- A computer program is a set of instructions.
- The instructions are stored on secondary storage, e.g. the hard disk.
- The instructions have to be copied into RAM before they can be carried out.

- The instructions are carried out by the processor.
- No processing takes place in RAM.

There are millions of different examples of software – a few examples are given on these pages.

System Software

System software controls the hardware. It's also used to create new software:

- **Operating systems** let us interact with the computer.
- **Editors** let us write program source code.

- **Compilers** change the program source code to machine code that the computer can run.
- **Loaders** copy programs from the hard disk into RAM.

Utilities

Utilities let us do maintenance jobs on the computer:

- **Defragmenters** let us clean up the disks, getting rid of wasted empty spaces.
- **Compression** software shrinks files, which makes it quicker to send them to someone else.
- **Anti-virus** software detects and gets rid of viruses that might damage our data.

- **Anti-malware** software can help prevent programs taking over our computer and doing things that we don't want.
- **Image editors** let us make changes to image files.
- **PDF** (portable document format) readers can display documents so that they exactly match the original.

Applications

Applications are programs that carry out the jobs that we want. Some applications are so universally useful that lots of people buy them. This makes them cheaper than having software specially written because the cost of development is shared across many customers. Common software like this is called **generic software**. Generic software is often very reliable because any faults are quickly spotted by the many users.

Examples of generic software include…
- word processors
- spreadsheets

- database management systems
- web browsers
- email
- image editors.

Some generic software is more specialised, but it still sells to lots of different people. For example…
- hotel booking software
- online ecommerce software
- software for making appointments at a doctor's surgery
- payroll
- stock control.

Specialised Software

Software is often specially written for a specific client or group of clients. This tends to be expensive and it may take a long time to get rid of bugs. Specialised software includes…

- air traffic control systems
- systems for running the London congestion charge
- systems for managing traffic on motorways.

Software also has to be written for specific types of electronic devices. There is software in…

- mobile phones
- MP3 players
- engine management systems
- autopilots
- traffic light controllers.

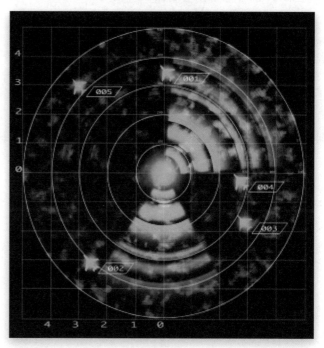

Air Traffic Control Radar

Open Source Versus Proprietary Software

Most software has to be paid for, and developing reliable software can be very expensive. Software owned by a person or company is called **proprietary software**. It is subject to copyright and there are restrictions on copying it.

A large number of PCs run Microsoft Windows™ and many people use Microsoft Office™ for producing documents. This has made Microsoft a very successful company.

Proprietary software is extremely valuable and the source code is a closely guarded secret.

Some software is developed by a worldwide community. They let anyone look at the source code. This is called **Open Source** software. For example:

- Linux operating system
- Mozilla Firefox
- Apache Web server

Quick Test

1. What is a computer program?
2. What software lets us control a computer?
3. What software cleans up empty spaces from a disk?
4. What is application software?

KEY WORDS
Make sure you understand these words before moving on!

- Operating system
- Editor
- Compiler
- Utilities
- Defragmenter
- Compression
- Application
- Generic software
- Proprietary software
- Open Source

Operating Systems

What is an Operating System?

An operating system is a set of programs that controls the computer hardware:

- It lets the user and the application software get results from the hardware.
- It means that the user doesn't need to understand the complicated workings of the computer.
- It allows programmers a short cut to the hardware. This makes it easier to write applications.

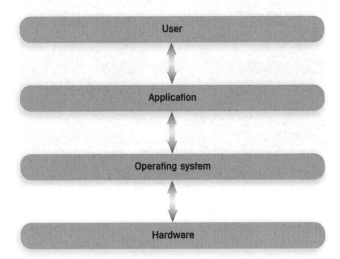

When a computer is switched on, the essential parts of the operating system are copied from backing store into RAM. This is called **booting**.

The operating system performs a huge range of different **tasks.** The following are some important examples:

- Saving data on storage devices.
- Retrieving data from storage devices.
- Managing data by allowing copying, deleting and renaming files.
- Sending jobs to the printer.
- Loading programs into memory.
- Protecting data in memory from being overwritten.
- Allowing software to access devices.
- Providing a user interface.

When a computer is switched on, the essential parts of the operating system are copied from backing store into RAM. This is called **booting**.

Device Drivers

Lots of devices are connected to a computer system, e.g. hard drives, video displays, keyboards and printers. Each device needs special instructions on how to carry out its tasks. These instructions come as **device drivers**.

The operating system works through device drivers to control the hardware. This makes it easy to add new equipment because only the drivers need to be added, not a new operating system.

Types of Operating System

Single User / Single Job	**Network**
The first PCs allowed just one program to run at a time. Nowadays, you will only see this 'single user / single job' system on dedicated computers, e.g. embedded systems.	Computer networks have special operating systems, which provide security and communication links. They also allow the network manager to keep on top of any problems.
Batch	**Real-time**
Mainframes allow the jobs and the data to be collected together and then run, with no further interaction. This is a **batch** system and it's useful in a situation where lots of data has to be processed in the same way, e.g. printing exam results.	When a computer responds immediately to input, this is called operating in **real-time.** Real-time operating is essential in… • computer games • autopilots • medical monitoring systems • most booking systems • traffic control systems.
Multiprogramming	**Interactive**
Most modern computers allow more than one program to be active in RAM at the same time. But, the processor can only act on one instruction at a time. A **multiprogramming** operating system lets the processor switch between jobs very fast so that it looks as if programs are being run at the same time.	Nowadays, people want to have a conversation with their computers – they expect to get an answer immediately. Modern PC operating systems are event-driven. This means that they wait for something to happen (e.g. a mouse click), then run the appropriate program code. This type of system is called **interactive.**

Quick Test

1. What software gives instructions to devices connected to the computer?
2. *Most PCs can run more than one program at the same time. True or false?*
3. What is real-time computing?
4. What is a batch process?

KEY WORDS

Make sure you understand these words before moving on!
- Device driver
- Batch
- Multiprogramming
- Real-time
- Interactive

Operating Systems

Operating Systems

You should be aware that there are lots of different operating systems. Remember that nowadays computers are very common, and the term 'computer' includes much more than just the PCs that sit on the table. Nearly all these different computers have operating systems.

Microsoft Windows™

Microsoft Windows™ is the most widely known operating system. It drives most of the PCs in the world. Over the years Windows has undergone many changes.

These changes have made it...
* more user friendly (in theory!)
* more capable (it can do more and more jobs with each upgrade)
* more complex (though some people think that it's far too complicated)
* more secure.

Windows™ is so complex that updates are issued regularly to fix problems and add new features. Most users let Windows do the **updates** automatically.

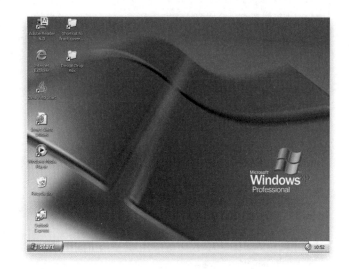

Other Operating Systems

Unix is a mainframe operating system that was developed along with the C programming language. It's still in widespread use in large installations.

Linux is an operating system like Unix, but it's Open Source. That means anyone can look at the source code and change it.

Mac OS is produced specifically for Apple computers.

Embedded systems often have their own operating systems that are sometimes integrated with the application.

Linux Operating System

Files

Files are named stores of data on a computer backing storage device. They can be any type of data at all, such as documents, spreadsheets, databases, music, images or programs.

Files can usually be given any name. It's important that you choose a name that has something to do with the data being stored.

File names also have **extensions.** These are extra parts added to the names to show what type of files they are. Applications look for extensions in order to find files that they can work with.

Examples in Windows™ systems:

Extension	File Type
doc	Word processed document
xls	Excel spreadsheet
pdf	Portable document format
htm	Web page

File names and extensions are often part of a **URL** (Uniform Resource Locator) that appears in a web browser. In the link below the file name is start.asp.

http://ipsum.org/folder1/start.asp

The complete location of a file is described in a **path.** The URL here shows a complete path. If you start at the ipsum.org website then look in the folder1 directory, you will find the file in there.

Directories (Folders)

Operating systems make it easy to group files together. They use **directories,** otherwise known as **folders,** to group files. Folders can be grouped within other folders. This is called a **hierarchical** system. It makes it easier to work with the computer.

Folders

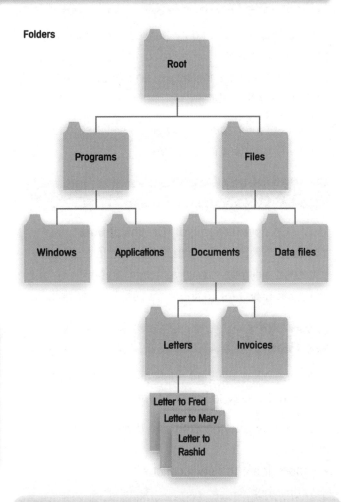

Quick Test

1. What is a computer file?
2. What is a folder?
3. What is a hierarchical directory?
4. What is a file extension?

KEY WORDS
Make sure you understand these words before moving on!
- Update
- Unix
- Linux
- File
- Extension
- URL
- Path
- Directory
- Folder
- Hierarchical

User Interfaces

Interfaces

An **interface** is a boundary between two things. A user interface is the boundary between the computer and the human. It's the way in which the human and the computer interact.

All sorts of interfaces have been developed and there will be more in the future.

Interfaces have been getting easier to use. There are big advantages in keeping interfaces similar. For example, it makes learning new applications easier.

The best interfaces are **intuitive.** This means that it's pretty obvious what to do.

GUI (Graphical User Interface)

Most PCs now have a **GUI (Graphical User Interface)**, which means that they can interact with users via pictures, known as **icons**. You click on an icon with a **pointer** (using a mouse or other pointing device) to select the process or file that you want. Or if you have a touch sensitive screen, you can touch the icon to select it. We now expect GUIs to have lots of features, which make controlling a computer easy.

Features of GUIs

Windows allow different applications to run side by side and it's easy to move between them.

In a window you can **drag and drop** items in order to...
- move them to new locations
- copy them
- delete them.

Windows can be moved or resized by dragging with the mouse. **Controls** such as buttons, check boxes and menus make it easy to learn new applications.

Dialogue boxes let you set lots of choices in one go, for example, setting print options.

Menus group similar choices together and may also have a toolbar, which allows you to click on a function that you want.

GUIs can be customized, so each user can choose colours and the size of icons, and the way that the GUI reacts. For example, people with impaired vision can enlarge the text and the icons.

A Set of Windows

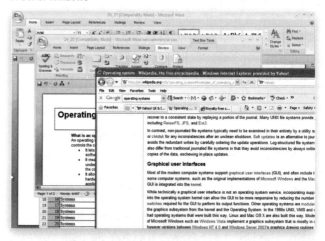

A Dialogue Box to Set Print Options

A Menu and Toolbar

User Interfaces

Hyperlinks and Hotspots

In many applications, especially web browsers, there are **hotspots** where clicking the mouse can take you to somewhere else.

These hotspots are supported by **hyperlinks** that connect to the target location or web page.

Other Interfaces

CLI (**Command Line Interface**) requires the user to type in commands.

CLIs are popular with expert users because they are quick, and commands can be grouped together to save time.

Menu Interfaces

Menu interfaces let the user make a choice and then this may lead to further choices. This is common in ATMs (cash machines).

Other Interfaces

Computers can be controlled by speaking to them and they can talk back, for example, car GPS systems can talk to you. This capability will improve in the future.

Specialist devices have their own interfaces, e.g. the controls of an aircraft.

Command Line Interface

```
C:\>cd drivers

C:\DRIVERS>dir
 Volume in drive C has no label.
 Volume Serial Number is E8BE-2D78

 Directory of C:\DRIVERS

01/05/2006  21:44    <DIR>          .
01/05/2006  21:44    <DIR>          ..
01/05/2006  21:44    <DIR>          AU
01/05/2006  21:46             4,128 IN
01/05/2006  21:44    <DIR>          NE
01/05/2006  21:44    <DIR>          SY
01/05/2006  21:44    <DIR>          vi
               1 File(s)          4,12
               6 Dir(s)  127,182,135,2
```

An ATM Menu Interface

Lonsdale Bank plc

Display Balance | Withdrawal with receipt
Change PIN | Withdrawal no receipt
Mobile Top-up | Cancel

Quick Test

1. What is an icon?
2. What input device would you use to drag and drop something?
3. What is a check box an example of?
4. What is the name of a box containing lots of choices that can be set together?

KEY WORDS

Make sure you understand these words before moving on!
- Interface
- Intuitive
- GUI
- Icon
- Pointer
- Drag and drop
- Control
- Dialogue box
- Menu
- Hotspot
- Hyperlink
- CLI

33

Teams

IT Jobs

Many people work in the IT industries. When you complete your **controlled assessment** in your ICT work, you often have to play the part of people who work as developers or support staff. It helps if you know that IT people usually work in teams and have different responsibilities.

In small organisations, different roles are often undertaken by the same person.

IT People

There's a shortage of good IT staff, so IT can be a good career choice.

But the best and most successful IT people aren't just good with computers. They also understand the business, can communicate well and are good at working with others.

These skills are often more important than just being a 'whizz' at coding.

The IT Team

The makeup of an IT team varies a great deal depending on the needs of an organisation. A possible structure might look like the following:

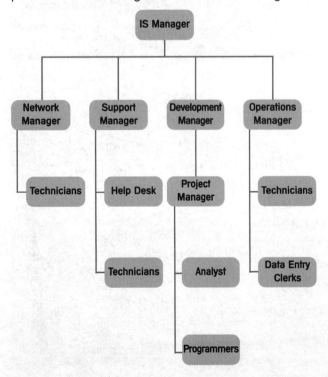

IS Manager

The **IS (Information Systems) manager** is responsible for deciding what IT systems an organisation needs. In many cases the IS manager is on the company's board and gets the business perspective from other board members.

Project Manager

The **project manager** takes charge of developing and implementing new systems, making sure that the right people are employed and that the system is produced on time, within budget and to an acceptable standard.

Operations Manager

An **operations manager** is in charge of the day-to-day running of the IT systems. Most big organisations concentrate their IT operations in a central data centre. Running this effectively is the operations manager's job.

The IT Team (Cont.)

Analyst

The **analyst** looks at the business and comes up with an IT solution. The analyst will often be involved in improving the system as it's being developed.

Programmer

The solution designed by the analyst is turned into a working program by a **programmer**, using a programming language or other methods.

Some or all of the solution can often be produced using automatic program-generating tools.

Technicians

Technicians are often junior members of the team and they carry out the installation, maintenance and repair work needed to keep the system running.

Network Manager

The network is so vital to most organisations that it will usually have its own team of people looking after it.

The **network manager** and team must make sure that the data is safe and that the system is available at all times.

User Support and Help Desk

It's vital that everyone in an organisation who works with information is able to keep working without computer problems.

There's usually a support team, led from the **help desk**, who respond to problems.

They have to assess incidents and decide whether to fix problems themselves or call in external help if the problem is too specialised.

Quick Test

1. Who is responsible for the direction of IT developments in an organisation?
2. What member of an IT team designs a solution to a business problem?
3. Describe one job performed by a help desk team.
4. Which team members do the actual installation and repair work?

KEY WORDS
Make sure you understand these words before moving on!
- Analyst
- Programmer
- Technicians
- Network manager
- Help desk

System Life Cycle

IT Projects

Making IT systems is not easy. Often they are entirely new ideas that have not been tried and tested before.

There's much room for misunderstanding because…
- it can be difficult for a software developer to accurately understand exactly what a client wants
- a customer may not always fully understand what an IT system can do.

Many IT projects go badly wrong. Huge amounts of money have been wasted on big IT projects that…
- have never been used
- went way over budget
- were unsuitable for the purpose.

To avoid costly disasters, sensible developers follow careful procedures to make sure that the clients get the systems that they want and are paying for.

Above all, the developers have to consult regularly with the clients to check that what they're producing is what is required.

The System Life Cycle

There are lots of well-tried methods for developers to follow in order to make sure that what they produce is what the client wants. These methods usually involve similar stages and can sometimes be represented as a **life cycle**:

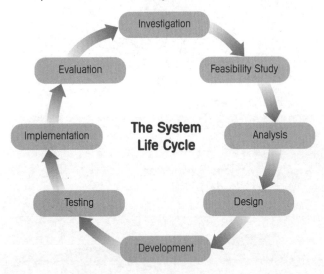

The System Life Cycle

Investigation → Feasibility Study → Analysis → Design → Development → Testing → Implementation → Evaluation → Investigation

Investigation

The developer has to undertake an **investigation** and look at the business problem and see what is going on at the moment. There are standard ways of doing this:
- **Interview:** it's necessary to talk to the people involved
- **Questionnaires:** these can be circulated to lots of people. The questions are all the same so the answers can be easily analysed.
- **Observation:** The investigator can look at work practices and the documentation that's used.

Feasibility Study

A **feasibility study** is used to see if the system is worthwhile and whether it can be achieved. Sometimes a project stops at this point if it's too expensive.

The System Life Cycle (Cont.)

Analysis

The developers do an **analysis** of a project and look at ways in which the system can be put together.

They make a list of what it must do – the **requirements specifications.**

Requirement Specifications

Design	The parts of the new system are planned, for example… • what it will look like • what processing must be done • how the data is to be organised.
Development (called **implementation** by some exam boards)	The system is produced by the programmers.
Testing	The system is no use if it goes wrong and has bugs in it. Testers will try to break the system to show any faults that need fixing. Testing by the developers is called **alpha testing**. Customers sometimes do some of the testing. This is called **beta testing**.
Implementation (otherwise called roll-out)	This is where the new system is installed for the customer. It might be installed all at once, or in stages. Sometimes it's run alongside the old system. This is called **parallel running.**
Evaluation	The system is checked against the original specifications.
Maintenance	Most systems need work after implementation. The customer's requirements may change or the system may still have some faults that need fixing.
Keeping in touch	The developers should keep in constant contact with the customer to make sure that what is being developed suits its purpose.

Quick Test

1. At which stage of the system life cycle is it decided whether or not to continue?
2. What is the purpose of testing a system?
3. What is parallel running?
4. What is program maintenance?

KEY WORDS

Make sure you understand these words before moving on!

- Life Cycle
- Investigation
- Feasibility Study
- Analysis
- Design
- Development
- Testing
- Implementation
- Evaluation
- Maintenance

Practice Questions

1 Which of the following is an example of system software? Tick the correct option.

   A A spreadsheet ◯   **B** A compiler ◯

   C A washing machine control program ◯   **D** Payroll processing ◯

2 Which of these is an operating system that allows more than one program to be resident in memory at the same time? Tick the correct option.

   A Multiplexing ◯   **B** Multiprogramming ◯

   C Multi user ◯   **D** Multitasking ◯

3 Fill in the missing words to complete the following sentences.

Software written by a worldwide community of unpaid volunteers is called _____

_____ . The software is _____ to users and they also have access

to the _____ _____ so that they can make changes if they want.

On the other hand, _____ software is owned by a company. For example the most

widely used PC operating system is _____ and it's owned by _____ .

4 Which of the following are applications? Tick the **three** correct options.

   A A word processor ◯   **B** A database management system ◯

   C An autopilot ◯   **D** A program editor ◯

   E A compiler ◯   **F** A program that manages memory ◯

5 Circle the correct options in the following sentences.

   a) A defragmenter is a **utility / device driver**.

   b) Program instructions are carried out in the **processor / RAM**.

   c) An interface where you can click on icons is a **CLI / GUI**.

   d) The person who's in charge of the day-to-day running of an IT system is an **analyst / operations manager**.

   e) A user with a computer fault should first ask for help from the **operations manager / help desk team**.

6 Choose the correct words from the options given to complete the following sentences.

   word processor   **web page**   **folder**   **extension**   **file**

A store of data on the hard disk is called a _____ and many of these are often

contained in a _____ . There are many types and they can sometimes be recognised

by the _____ , which is a group of letters after their name. For example, if you see the

letters 'doc', you will expect this to have been produced by a _____ . 'htm' refers to a

_____ .

7 What is it called when data is collected together and then processed by the computer in one session? Tick the correct option.

A An interactive process ⬭

B A real-time process ⬭

C A multi-tasking process ⬭

D A batch process ⬭

8 Choose the correct words from the options given to complete the following sentences.

| users | bugs | spreadsheet | testing | inexpensive |

A .... is an example of generic software. It tends to be relatively

.... because it's bought by many .... Sometimes, software

must be specially written for an organisation that has a unique problem. This software takes longer to

produce and may have .... in it when it's delivered because it hasn't had enough

....

9 Which of the following might be found in a dialogue box? Tick the **three** correct options.

A A command button ⬭   **B** A mouse button ⬭

C The Enter key ⬭   **D** A drop-down list box ⬭

E A check box ⬭   **F** A USB port ⬭

10 Fill in the missing words to complete the following sentences.

An .... is the boundary between the user and the .... If it's

easy to use, it's called .... You use a .... to click on an

.... in order to access the software that you want.

11 Explain why a new computer system may require maintenance.

....

....

....

....

Data and Information

Data

Data is just facts:

- It's made from symbols.
- It simply exists.
- It has no meaning.

In the real world, data can be almost anything.

None of the items of data in the table actually mean anything in themselves. But, if you know the **context,** then the data can start to be useful.

Computers just manipulate data according to the rules we give them. They do not understand the data.

Data	What It Might Mean
yes no no no yes	Whether to admit each person to the night club
(musical notation)	Music to your ears
(barcode) 3 850289 001369	A tin of beans
23-34-45	A bank sort code
1101000011100000	A computer instruction SHL AL,1

Information

Data becomes **information** when it has context. If we know what the data items refer to, then we can make use of them.

Computers are good at handling data – for them, all data is a stream of **bits.** What they do with these bits depends on the software that's being used.

Input to a computer can be regarded as data. Output from a computer might be data for another system or it might be information that humans can use.

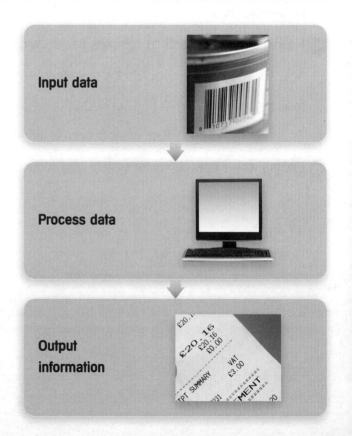

Input data

Process data

Output information

Finding Information

Nowadays, it's easy to find information about practically anything on the Internet. If you go to any search engine, you will be able to find something about what you want.

But, the Internet is not necessarily always the best place to look. There are advantages and disadvantages to finding information on the Internet.

Advantages:
- It may be very up-to-date.
- It may come from the best experts in their field.
- It may be in multi-media format and easy to understand.
- There are lots of alternative sources such as websites, **blogs**, microblogs, **wikis**, **podcasts**, discussion boards and social networking sites.
- You can discuss information with others.

Disadvantages:
- It may be old information.
- Anyone can put information online so it may be unreliable.
- It may be badly presented.
- A blog is often just a set of opinions.
- A discussion may or may not be useful to you.

In the past, we would often rely on printed or broadcast material being carefully prepared and reviewed before it was published. Now, we should be more careful and suspicious because we know that information online may be biased or have some 'spin' to persuade us of someone's point of view.

There are a few things that give some indication of how reliable online information is, for example, by looking at the domain name. But in the end, you have to be careful and exercise judgment.

Don't forget that there are other sources of information still available, for example…
- the printed word
- DVDs
- CDs
- images
- maps
- conversations
- radio and television.

Quick Test

1. What is data?
2. What makes data into information?
3. Which is likely to be more up-to-date – a newspaper article or an Internet news page?
4. How does a computer input data about a product in a supermarket?

KEY WORDS
Make sure you understand these words before moving on!
- Data
- Context
- Information
- Bit
- Blog
- Wiki
- Podcast

Document Processing

Presenting Information

A computer will **process** information in any way that we program it to. The reason for processing information is to get **output.** The output is usually information for humans to use.

A lot of care has to go into presenting information so that the target audience can understand it. Because of this, some of the most common software is designed to help us display information clearly.

Documents

Maybe one day we will stop needing paper documents – but not yet. Computers have produced more paper output than we ever had before.

We still need printed copies of output...
*   for legal evidence
*   to read when away from a computer.

Computers have made it easy to produce attractive and clear documents. Even if you don't have any design skills, by selecting the **default** options that are set by common software applications you can still be sure of a reasonable result.

Modern software makes it easy to combine information from lots of sources into one document. We would find it hard to create some documents without **copy and paste**.

Document Processing Software

As with any job, it's best to use the right tools in order to get the best results.

Editor

A **text editor** is what you need if you want to save just the words you type and nothing else, i.e. you just want **ASCII** characters but don't need formatting, bold, italic, tables, etc.

You would use a text editor if you are writing program code or are editing the HTML of a web page.

Word Processor

Most people use a **word processor** for document processing. Nearly everyone who works or plays on a computer needs one. Word processors have developed a wide range of features that make it easy to produce well-presented documents:
*   Different fonts have different impacts.
*   Words can be formatted in different ways, e.g. **bold,** *italic* and <u>underlined</u>.
*   **Templates** can be used to automate the production of common document types, e.g. newsletters or certificates.

Text Editor

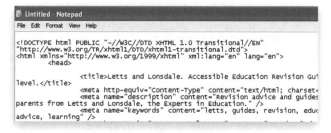

Templates

Document Processing Software (Cont.)

Different fonts can be selected:
- A sans serif font has no tags on the letters.
- A serif font has tags on the letters and is often used for long passages.

Sans Serif Font

Lorem ipsum dolor sit amet, consectetur adipiscing elit. Suspendisse posuere posuere orci nec hendrerit. Proin euismod elit id nisi vehicula fermentum.

Serif Font

Lorem ipsum dolor sit amet, consectetur adipiscing elit. Suspendisse posuere posuere orci nec hendrerit. Proin euismod elit id nisi vehicula fermentum.

Track changes lets you see all the changes that have been made to a document. **Comments** means that you can add text adjacent to the main text. Both these functions help you to work with others.

Track Changes

Lorem ipsum dolor sit amet, consectetur adipiscing elit. Suspendisse posuere posuere orci nec hendrerit. Proin euismod elit id nisi vehicula fermentum. Donec quis nisl ac est volutpat aliquam id non ante. Curabitur nibh iaculis in ullamcorper accumsan sem nec nibh fermentum a dapibus nisi semper. Nunc turpis quam, lobortis vehicula feugiat sit amet, sodales vitae erat. Sed pretium auctor arcu eget cursus. Aliquam non luctus justo.

Comment [S1]: I don't agree with this – better to consult the MD]

The **spell checker** is very useful even if you are good at spelling. It lets you type faster without worrying about making typo errors. The spell checker looks up words in a dictionary and lets you know if you have typed a word that isn't recognised.

But, they don't stop all errors.

> Eye no that this is rite four the checker tolled me sew.

The **word count** feature is useful in order to give you an estimate of how much text might fit on a page or if you need to know the total number of words in a passage or document.

Word Count

You can also...
- number pages automatically
- create contents and index pages
- add images
- create footnotes
- automate tasks with macros.

Quick Test

1. What software would you use to edit the HTML of a web page?
2. What is a default option?
3. What is the feature of a word processor that gives you a design for a new document such as a newsletter?
4. What does the track changes option on a word processor do?

KEY WORDS

Make sure you understand these words before moving on!
- Process
- Default
- Copy and paste
- Text editor
- ASCII
- Word processor
- Template
- Track changes
- Comments
- Spell checker
- Word count

Document Processing

Mail Merge

Mail merge can be used if you want to send the same document to lots of people but with some details changed, for example the name and address. This application lets you put in fields that are filled in from a database when the document is printed.

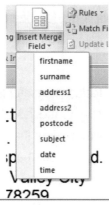

Vector Graphics

Word processors allow you to create quite sophisticated drawings very easily. Vector graphics can be produced, which can be enlarged properly.

Pictures such as photographs and other bit-mapped images can be imported and arranged into layers so that they overlap each other.

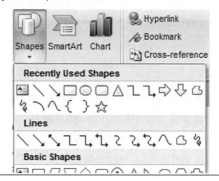

Headers / Footers

Headers / Footers let you have the same reference on each page. You can also add automatic page numbering.

Tables

Tables are useful for most page layout situations. Turning the gridlines on allows you to see what you are doing.

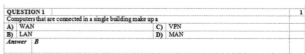

Search and Replace

Search and replace can be used to make changes throughout a document. For example...

- you might want to change someone's name
- you might want to enter an abbreviation and then change it throughout the document to the correct wording later on. This saves effort.

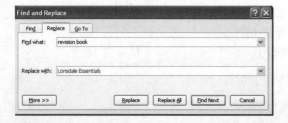

Print Preview

Print preview lets you see how a document looks before you print it. This allows you to make sure that it looks how you want it to before you use up paper printing it.

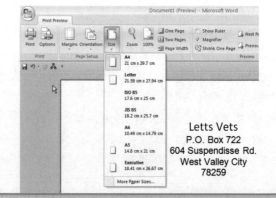

Macros and Consistent Layout

A **macro** can be set up if you need to perform the same action many times. This is a small program that you can either write in a programming language or you can simply carry out the actions and record the steps.

A macro is useful…

- to save effort
- to make sure that things are done consistently (e.g. documents from organisations have to be in a **house style** to give the right impression)
- for things that need to be done lots of times.

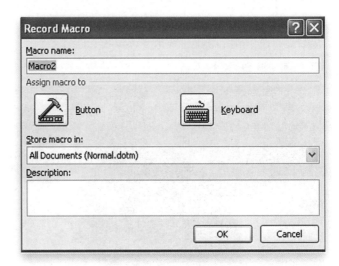

Desk Top Publishing Software

Word processors can be used for most ordinary document work, but they're not really designed for sophisticated page layouts.

If the layout is the main focus of the document production, then **DTP** (Desk Top Publishing) software is needed. DTP has all sorts of features that let you control the exact look of the page.

DTP is fully **WYSIWYG** (What You See is What You Get). For example, this revision guide was written using a word processor, but the pages were laid out using DTP software.

Quick Test

1. What is the section at the bottom of every page called?
2. How do you check that a page is looking right before you print it?
3. What is a small program that you can record in a word processor and replay it whenever you want?
4. What do you call the standard look of documents that comes from an organisation?

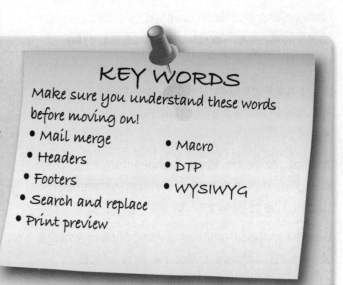

KEY WORDS

Make sure you understand these words before moving on!

- Mail merge
- Headers
- Footers
- Search and replace
- Print preview
- Macro
- DTP
- WYSIWYG

Graphics

Bit-mapped Graphics

Computers can represent pictures as sets of dots or **pixels**. A picture created in this way is called a **bit-mapped graphic.**

At its simplest, a dot can be switched on or off. This allows a black and white image to be produced.

The more dots there are, the higher the **resolution** of the picture. A picture with a high resolution will be clearer than a picture with a low resolution.

Close up, the dots are quite obvious.

From a distance, the dots don't show as obviously.

In a colour picture, more bits are needed to represent each pixel. For a high resolution colour image, this can lead to huge file sizes.

Digital photographs are bit-mapped images. From a camera with a high count of megapixels, the file size can be too big to upload to some sites, e.g. social networking or picture sharing, so the files have to be **compressed.**

Imaging Software

Images are easy to change when they're in a bit-mapped form. There are lots of **image editors** available to produce effects such as changing colours and transforming images in various ways.

Although images can be changed for artistic purposes, image editors can also be used by criminals, for example by altering images for passport photographs.

Some graphics software is so good that it can be impossible to tell if a transformed image is genuine or not.

Images can be gradually changed from an original to another different image, showing intermediate stages. This is called **morphing**.

Most bit-mapped graphics packages have a range of tools that achieve a wide range of effects.

Transformed Bit-mapped Image of Cat – Mosaic Effect

Vector Graphics

Bit-mapped graphics don't enlarge well because the pixels start to show.

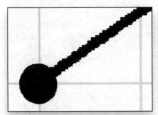

Bit-mapped zoom

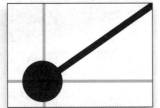

Vector graphics zoom

Instead, some images are represented by mathematical formulae instead of a set of bits. These formulae can be rendered into an image with the right software. **Vector graphics** can be useful for animated films.

The graphics that come with a word processor are vector based and will enlarge properly.

Vector graphics are useful when you don't want lots of unnecessary detail such as the detail you might get in a photograph. Vectors are used in…

* architects' plans
* engineering drawings
* video displays on web pages.

Some file types used on web pages such as SWF (Small Web Format or Shockwave Flash) are used to store vector-based animations. These animations can be enlarged to fit any size of monitor without the pixellation that bit-mapped graphics would suffer.

Vector Graphic

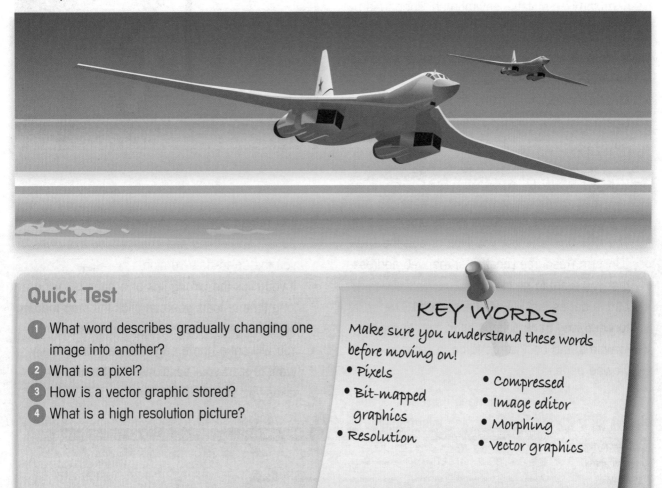

Quick Test

1. What word describes gradually changing one image into another?
2. What is a pixel?
3. How is a vector graphic stored?
4. What is a high resolution picture?

KEY WORDS

Make sure you understand these words before moving on!

* Pixels
* Bit-mapped graphics
* Resolution
* Compressed
* Image editor
* Morphing
* Vector graphics

Software for the Web

Viewing the Web

The World Wide Web is made up of billions of web pages on billions of web sites. You can look at any site or page that you want because the web is **standardised**. This means that all the web pages have to be made in a certain way so they will display properly on our computers.

The basic standard for web page construction is the description language HTML (**Hypertext Markup Language**). HTML has all sorts of capabilities built in that allow it to work with other standards, but each page has to have an HTML basis.

The basic requirement to view a web page is a web **browser**. A browser takes HTML code and transforms it into a screen display. It also has the ability to run programs linked to the web page, provided they have been written in a suitable environment supported by the browser.

There are several popular browsers in use, for example...
- Internet Explorer
- Mozilla Firefox
- Opera
- Safari

Features Offered by Browsers

There are some basic operations that all browsers offer.
- The **URL** box is where you type or add the URL (Uniform Resource Locator) of the web address that you want to go to.
- All the pages that you visit are stored. The **forward and back** buttons allow you to move forwards and backwards to go to recently viewed pages.

- The **reload** operation allows you to refresh a page if something has changed, so this gives you the up-to-date version.
- If you click the wrong link or a page is taking a long time to load, you can click the **stop loading** button. This will stop a page from loading.
- You will set a home page where you normally want to start your sessions. The **home** button takes you straight back there.

①	URL box
②	Backwards
③	Forwards
④	Reload
⑤	Stop loading
⑥	Home button

Features Offered by Browsers (Cont.)

The pages you visited in the past are stored so that you can revisit them quickly. This is called the **history**.

You may want to clear your history from time to time to stop others seeing what sites you have looked at.

History

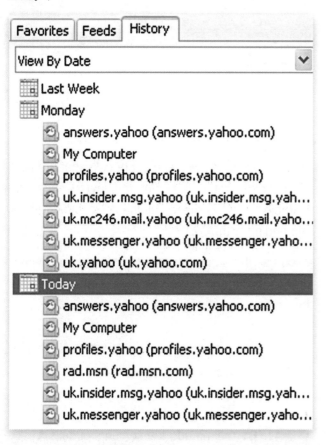

A variety of **toolbars** can be attached to your browser. These give one-click access to common functions. Some toolbars are specially supplied by third parties. The picture opposite shows the Google toolbar.

Multimedia platforms – all web browsers support the playing of multimedia files in the browser window. Examples include…
- Flash™
- Real Player™
- Quicktime™

Hemera / Thinkstock

Quick Test

1. What is a URL?
2. What do you do if you want to return to the last page you visited on the web during a session?
3. What is a toolbar used for?
4. Why might you click the **stop loading** button?

KEY WORDS

Make sure you understand these words before moving on!
- HTML
- Browser
- URL
- History
- Toolbar
- Multimedia platform

Spreadsheets

Spreadsheets

Spreadsheets are one of the most widely used types of generic software. They can be used to manipulate data in a huge number of ways. Although they're mostly used to 'crunch numbers', they can be used to organise any data.

Spreadsheets are made up of lots of **cells,** which are boxes arranged in a grid. Spreadsheets have **rows** labelled with numbers and **columns** labelled with letters.

Each cell has its own **address** or coordinates. The top left cell is A1; the next one down from there is A2 and so on.

The boxes can contain any type of data:

- Numbers
- Text (sometimes referred to as a label)
- Dates and times

A Spreadsheet

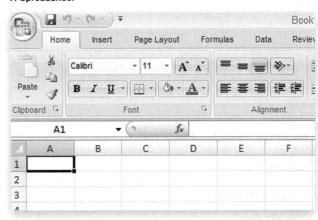

Ranges

It's often useful to refer to a set of cells that are next to each other. You use a colon to show a **range.** For example, (A1:A12) means all the cells starting at A1 and ending with A12.

If you use the same range a lot or if you don't want to keep looking up where the data is, you can name the range.

Formulae and Functions

You can put **formulae** and **functions** into a spreadsheet cell. This is where the power of spreadsheets comes from. The formulae and functions can refer to other cells. Formulae and functions all start with the equals sign. That way the spreadsheet software knows to perform an action and not just display the data.

Formulae

Formulae use operators to link cells and values together. There are many operators but common ones are signs like…

- + (plus)
- − (minus)
- * (multiply)
- / (divide)
- ^(raise to the power of).

For example:

- **=A1+B1** means add the contents of cells A1 and B1 together.
- **=A12/B15** means divide the content of A12 by the content of B15.

You can put numbers into formulae:

- **=A12^2** means the contents of A12 squared.
- **=A1+1** means take the value in A1 and add 1 to it.

You can use brackets to enforce the order of a calculation:

- **=(A1+1)*(A2+2)** means work out the value of A1 plus 1, then work out the value of A2 plus 2, then multiply the results together.

Formulae and Functions (Cont.)

Functions

Functions are applications (often calculations) that do lots of useful things, e.g. working out the average of a list of numbers. Functions have been pre-set so all the steps are automatically carried out. You just need to select the data you want to process and click the required function button.

There are lots of functions supplied with spreadsheets, but you can always write your own if you need a function that hasn't been included.

One of the most common functions is called SUM.

- **=SUM(A12:B30)** means add up all the values in the range of cells starting at A12 and finishing at B30.

If you had named that range 'data' you could have entered **=SUM(data).**

If you want the average of the range of cells you can use **=AVERAGE(A12:B30).**

The IF function lets you get the spreadsheet to make choices, For example, **=IF(B10>=50, "PASS","FAIL")** means if the value in B10 is greater than or equal to 50 then display the word PASS, otherwise display the word FAIL.

There are useful functions for...
- looking up data **(VLOOKUP)**
- finding the maximum in a range **(MAX)**
- working out interest payments **(ACCRINT).**

Look up a few of these functions on your spreadsheet software.

Choosing a Function

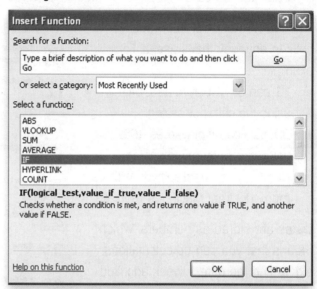

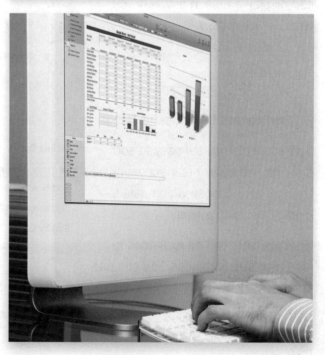

Copy and Cell Addressing

If you copy a formula from one place to another, it will adjust to reflect its new position.

For example, if you copy **=A1*B20** one cell down, it will now say **=A2*B21**. Although this is usually what you want to happen, you might sometimes want to always refer to the same cell.

For example, if the tax rate is in cell B20, you might always want a formula to multiply a sum by the tax rate. You use **absolute cell addressing** to do that. So, if you enter **=A1*B20**, the B20 reference will not change if you copy the formula. The dollar signs mean 'don't change this'. Alternatively, you could give the tax cell a name and refer to that.

Spreadsheets

Formatting Cells

Data and Dates

You can **format** or arrange data in cells in any way that's useful. For example:

- 1.1 can be displayed as £1.10 using the currency setting.
- 0.1 can be displayed as 10% using the percentage setting.
- Numbers can be displayed with as many decimal places as required.

Dates are stored as numbers, which means that you can do calculations, e.g. to find the date 1 week ago. You can display a date in any way you want, for example…

- 12 May 2010
- 12/5/2010
- 5/12/2010 (American)

Formatting Data Box

ABC 123	General — No specific format
12	Number
	Currency
	Accounting
	Short Date
	Long Date
	Time
%	Percentage
½	Fraction
10²	Scientific

Formatting Dates

Format Cells

Tabs: Number | Alignment | Font | Border | Fill

Category:
General
Number
Currency
Accounting
Date
Time
Percentage
Fraction
Scientific
Text
Special
Custom

Sample

Type:
*14/03/2001
*14 March 2001
14/03/2001
14/03/01
14/3/01
14.3.01
2001-03-14

Locale (location):
English (U.K.)

Sorting and Other Useful Things

Spreadsheets make it easy to **sort** data into whatever order you want. You can also choose which data to display by using a **filter**.

Spreadsheets can be expanded to whatever size is needed. You can use spreadsheets to easily summarise data. You can group blocks of data and analyse them easily by using a **pivot table**.

The spreadsheet opposite shows lots of data from different sales people who sold items on different days. This detail is recorded in a flat spreadsheet, and the data can be easily summarised using a pivot table.

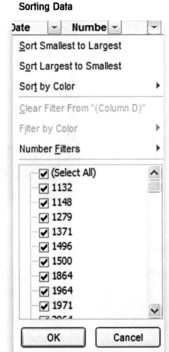

Sorting Data

Date ▾	Numbe ▾	▾

Sort Smallest to Largest

Sort Largest to Smallest

Sort by Color ▸

Clear Filter From "(Column D)"

Filter by Color ▸

Number Filters ▸

☑ (Select All)
☑ 1132
☑ 1148
☑ 1279
☑ 1371
☑ 1496
☑ 1500
☑ 1864
☑ 1964
☑ 1971

[OK] [Cancel]

Flat Spreadsheet

	A	B	C	D
1	Name	Date	Number	
2	Erich	30/08/2010	9585	2305
3	Erich	29/08/2010	2269	1500
4	Erich	28/08/2010	7674	4223
5	Erich	27/08/2010	5078	7376
6	Erich	28/08/2010	3352	9902
7	Erich	26/08/2010	8720	9474
8	Erich	27/08/2010	9902	4456
9	Erich	29/08/2010	3072	4120
10	Erich	27/08/2010	7647	9502
11	Megan	29/08/2010	3346	7675
12	Megan	29/08/2010	6083	7259
13	Megan	29/08/2010	6009	8528
14	Megan	26/08/2010	4094	6201
15	Megan	26/08/2010	4747	1279
16	Megan	27/08/2010	2943	3631

Pivot Table

16	⊟ Erich	57299
17	26/08/2010	8720
18	27/08/2010	22627
19	28/08/2010	11026
20	29/08/2010	5341
21	30/08/2010	9585
22	⊟ Megan	81606
23	26/08/2010	21678

Graphs

Another way to summarise data is to use a graph or chart. There are lots of ways of making different charts using spreadsheets.

Graphs can be embedded in word-processed documents. They can be linked to the data, so if it changes, the chart in the document gets updated.

Macros

You can record or write **macros** in spreadsheets just as you can in word processors.

Macros save effort and can make formatting or generating charts a one-click process.

Modelling and What If...?

A **model** is a mathematical representation of reality. Models can be created easily using spreadsheets.

You can use formulae and functions to model some situations, for example, the exchange rates for different currencies. You could then plan a holiday on a spreadsheet and if the rates change, you can easily get the sheet to recalculate the projected costs.

You might then ask the question 'what if the exchange rate goes up?'. The spreadsheet will be able to give you this information.

Quick Test

1. What is **=AVERAGE(B1:B10)** an example of?
2. What is **(B1:B10)** an example of?
3. What is an operator in a spreadsheet?
4. What would **=MAX(A1:A12)** do?
5. What would happen if the formula **=A1*B1** were copied to a new location?
6. How is a date stored in a spreadsheet?
7. State two ways in which data can be summarised on a spreadsheet.
8. What is a spreadsheet model?

KEY WORDS

Make sure you understand these words before moving on!

- Cell
- Row
- Column
- Address
- Range
- Formula
- Function
- Absolute cell addressing
- Format
- Pivot table
- Recalculate
- What if?

Presentations

What are Presentations?

Presentations are **multimedia** displays of information.

Presentations are used to…
- help communicate with a group
- advertise something
- provide public information displays.

Multimedia

A multimedia presentation is one that includes at least two of the following:
- Text
- Graphics
- Movies
- **Animations**
- Sound

A multimedia presentation can look quite exciting and is more likely to hold the audience's attention compared to a simple presentation just involving written or spoken text.

But, many presentations are just made from a series of slides and since this format is now very common it can tend to be boring.

Presentation Software

Presentation software allows you to make a set of slides. The slides can be static or multimedia. It's possible to bring together data from other applications so that you can have text and graphs as well as movies and sounds.

Presentations are usually projected onto a screen. Some presentations are left running in a public place so that people can see…
- a demonstration of a product
- what an institution does, e.g. schools often have presentations running on open days.

Transitions and Animations

Slide shows can be made more interesting by having…
- each slide merge into the next using some **transition** effect like dissolve or wipe across
- the words drop in or fly from the side.

But, overuse of these **animation** effects can be irritating.

Templates

Even if you don't have a lot of design knowledge or skills, you can use a **template** to help create a presentation that looks attractive and professional.

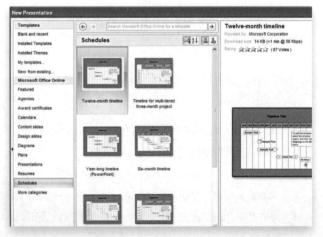

Notes

Presentation software lets you make copies of the slides and add notes so that the people watching can take away a copy.

Good Design

Although computer software has made it very easy to put together a presentation, you still need to make sure that any presentation you put together is interesting and well thought out. There's an expression 'Death by Powerpoint' that sums up how bad some presentations can be! So, you should think about the content and information that you are trying to convey.

Consistency

It's usually a good idea if there is a common design throughout a show. **Master slides** let you repeat material on every slide, for example…

* logos
* the name of the company.

Fitness for Purpose

Care needs to be taken to suit the presentation to the audience. For example, it's not relevant to include lots of intricate detail in a presentation to a company's board of directors who just want an overview.

Style Points

There are some simple style points to follow to help put together a good presentation:

* Don't put too much information on a slide.
* Don't simply read out what is on the slide.
* Choose colours that work together.
* Don't overuse graphics or gimmicks.
* Don't make too many slides.

How to make a bad presentation

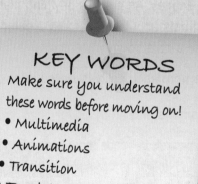

* don't be consistent
* use lots colours
* choose a bad background colour
* write far too much boring text on the screen so that people can't be bothered to read it
* add pointless graphics
* put them in strange places

Quick Test

1. What is a slide transition?
2. What is a multimedia presentation?
3. How do you automatically put something on every slide?
4. What is a ready-made presentation design called?

KEY WORDS

Make sure you understand these words before moving on!

* Multimedia
* Animations
* Transition
* Template
* Master slide

Databases

Databases

Databases are probably the most important application of computers. They underpin most of the things that computers are used for. Processing databases is what computers are particularly good at.

Databases are organised stores of data on a computer system. Because the data is organised, it can be processed by automatic systems.

Databases are used in many ways that make our modern life possible.

For example, without databases we would not have…
- online shopping
- social networking
- mobile phones
- banking (in its present form)
- online booking systems
- automated payroll.

Databases come in different forms.

Flat File Database

A **flat file database** is a simple database that can be created with a spreadsheet or even a word-processed table as well as with a database management system.

In the flat file database shown here, each row is called a **record** and each column is a **field.** There are four fields and nine records.

Flat file databases are rather limited and aren't very flexible. They're suitable for simple applications, such as creating an address book.

	A	B	C	D	E	F
1	First name	Surname	DOB	email		
2	Flynn	Hansen	31/10/86	In.scelerisque@nequenonquam.org		
3	Quail	Dillon	21/06/83	imperdiet@NulladignissimMaecenas.ca		
4	Basia	Donaldson	08/03/95	ac@magnaNam.ca		
5	Raja	Stephens	15/06/81	eget@miAliquamgravida.org		
6	Chadwick	Vincent	07/05/80	mi.lorem.vehicula@dis.edu		
7	April	Church	05/07/99	egestas.Sed.pharetra@luctusvulputate.org		
8	Cruz	Fernandez	25/10/93	eget.volutpat@Donecnibh.org		
9	Vance	Booth	19/01/00	ac.orci@etipsumcursus.ca		
10	Tatum	Lester	02/02/88	odio.semper@necmalesuada.org		

Relational Databases

The most common type of database is a **relational database.** This type separates the data from different **entities**. An entity is anything that you want to collect data about, for example, a person, an invoice or a hotel room.

The data from each entity is stored in a separate **table.**

Each table has a **key field.** The key field is unique to each record and is used to identify each record.

The tables are linked by key fields, which are usually ID numbers, chosen so that they're all different.

The database below shows 4 tables, which contain the details of landlords, their properties, lettings and tenants.

Relational Databases (Cont.)

By storing data about different things in separate tables, most data is stored once only. This avoids **data redundancy,** which is where lots of copies of the same data are made and they end up being inconsistent.

Forms are used to make a user-friendly interface with the database.

Queries can be set up to extract the data that is needed.

Reports are printed results from queries.

Database Form

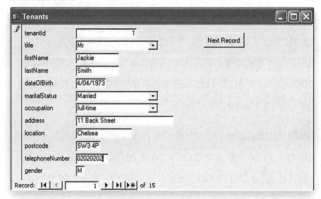

Database Software

Programmers write applications in order to keep control of and search databases. This job is made easier when the database is under the control of a **database management system** (DBMS). A DBMS like Microsoft Access™ or Oracle Database™ lets the programmers write new applications without having to worry about managing the precise way in which the data is stored.

Database Application 1   **Database Application 2**

DBMS

Database

Some DBMS systems have **wizards,** which are tools to help you make forms and other objects automatically.

Wizard

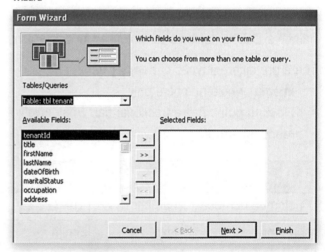

Quick Test

1 What is the software that organises the data in a database?
2 What is a key field?
3 What is an entity?
4 What is a relational database?

KEY WORDS

Make sure you understand these words before moving on!

- Flat file database
- Record
- Field
- Relational database
- Entity
- Table
- Key field
- Data redundancy
- Query
- Report
- Form
- Database management system
- Wizard

Databases

Data Types

To a computer, all data is binary. So, this means that we need to decide what the data should mean to humans. It's easier if we use different types of data because it becomes easier for us to organise and understand. We can also invent rules that help us not to make mistakes.

Data types are conventions that help us and although some are pretty well established, they do vary a little between systems. When you set up a data table, you need to decide what type of data each field will contain.

Different Types of Data

Alphabetic data takes letters.

Alphanumeric / text / string data takes letters and numbers. But the numbers can't be used for calculations.

There are different types of **number** data.
- **Integer:** whole numbers only
- **Floating point:** has a fractional part (may involve rounding errors).

Currency is a special format that gives two decimal places for money amounts.

Boolean or **Yes / No** is data that can take either the value **true** or **false.** This is sometimes represented as 1 or 0.

A **date** is often stored as a number but is displayed and input in any date format that the user wishes.

Field name	Data type	Example data	Explanation
Customer_number	number	1147	A unique number – primary key field.
surname	text	Smith	Letters only needed.
forename	text	John	Letters only needed.
date of birth	date	12/3/78	Date can be displayed in different ways but it's stored in the same way.
gender	text	m	One letter required. This isn't Boolean as it isn't **true** or **false.**
telephone	text	+4499999	Not a number because it may contain signs, spaces or leading zeroes.
email	text	ac@magnam.ca	Text allows symbols such as @.
credit_limit	number	10000	We need a number so we can do comparisons. Currency is also acceptable.
in_employment	boolean	true	Yes or no answer.

Querying a Database

One of the great advantages of using databases is that you can extract only the information you require. There is usually a **query language** to help you make the queries.

With online databases, such as those used by search engines, there are often similarities. You must always be precise otherwise you will not get the information you require.

When querying a database we use **operators** like the following:

Operator	Meaning
=	equals
>	greater than
<	less than
>=	greater than or equal to
<=	less than or equal to

For example, if we wanted a list of names for all the customers who are in work, we can write a query like this:

- SELECT surname, forename WHERE in_employment=true

We can combine conditions with AND, OR and NOT.

For example, if we wanted a list of names for all the customers who are in work **and** have a credit limit of more than 5000, we can write a query like this:

- SELECT surname, forename WHERE credit_limit>5000 AND in_employment=true

The framing of questions in search engines will involve different words and techniques but the use of linking words will be the same.

Using a Query Language to Handle a Database

```
CREATE TABLE OrderProduct (
    OrderID SMALLINT NOT NULL,
    ProductID SMALLINT NOT NULL,

    PRIMARY KEY (OrderID, ProductID),
    FOREIGN KEY (OrderID) REFERENCES Orders
(OrderID),
    FOREIGN KEY (ProductID) REFERENCES Products
(ProductID)
)
ENGINE=INNODB;


INSERT INTO OrderProduct VALUES  (1001, 16754),
                                 (1002, 18765),
                                 (1003, 18765),
                                 (1009, 19654),
                                 (1011, 18654),
                                 (1013, 19655),
                                 (1015, 19327),
                                 (1016, 17654);


SELECT ProductName, ProductID FROM Products,
OrderProduct;
```

Quick Test

1. What word do we use in a query to select data that combines two conditions?
2. What data type can only take the values true or false?
3. What data type is suitable for a postcode?
4. What data type is for whole numbers only?

KEY WORDS

Make sure you understand these words before moving on!
- Alphabetic
- Alphanumeric
- Text
- String
- Integer
- Floating point
- Boolean
- Query language
- Operator

Data Capture

What is Data Capture?

Data capture is the collection of data from the real world for input to a computer system.

Data capture can be divided into either **human** or **automatic** methods. Human methods are avoided if possible because they are…

- slow
- prone to error.

But sometimes human methods can't be avoided. For example, data has to be manually keyed in when…

- data is provided on a paper form
- observations are made.

Forms

Data capture forms can be on paper or on screen. They are designed to collect information from human users.

It's important to design **forms** carefully so that you get exactly the information you need.

A well-designed form uses tick boxes, character boxes and other helpful features to make sure that the information is exactly right for processing.

On-screen forms make use of controls such as **drop-down boxes** to help get the right information.

Personal Information			
NAME (LAST NAME FIRST)		SOCIAL SECURITY NO.	
ADDRESS	CITY	STATE	ZIP CODE
PHONE NO. ( )		REFERRED BY	

Employment Desired

POSITION	DATE YOU CAN START	SALARY DESIRED
ARE YOU EMPLOYED? ☐ Yes ☐ No	IF SO, MAY WE INQUIRE OF YOUR PRESENT EMPLOYER? ☐ Yes ☐ No	
EVER APPLIED TO THIS COMPANY BEFORE? ☐ Yes ☐ No	WHERE?	WHEN?

Education History

	NAME OF SCHOOL	YEARS ATTENDED	SUBJECTS STUDIED	DIPLOMA/DEGREE
GRAMMAR SCHOOL				
HIGH SCHOOL				
COLLEGE				
TRADE, BUSINESS OR CORRESPONDENCE SCHOOL				

General Information

SUBJECTS OF SPECIAL STUDY, WORK, OR SPECIAL TRAINING & SKILLS

Validation and Verification

Validation is the checking of data as it's being input to make sure it conforms to certain rules. This reduces the number of data entry errors, but it doesn't ensure that data is correct, only that it's in an acceptable format.

Verification means making sure that data is correct. The data may be compared with the source or sometimes two people type in the same data and the computer checks that the data is the same.

Some Methods of Validation

The following are some methods of validation:

- **Range check:** the data must be between limits.
- **Type check:** the data must be the correct data type, e.g. numbers.
- **Presence check:** a mandatory field, i.e. there must be something there.
- **Check digit:** a calculation produces an extra digit – the digit must match when the data is input. Bar codes have check digits.
- **Existence check:** the data must match some pre-existing data item, for example, an account number that exists. Drop-down boxes can look up allowable data in a list.

Automated Data Entry

It's more reliable to get a machine to enter data because machines rarely make mistakes.

Common methods of automated data entry include the following:

- **Chip and PIN** – the smart card is read by machine to identify the card.
- **OMR (Optical Mark Recognition)** – used for lottery ticket entry and examination answer sheets.
- **Bar codes** – used to identify many items such as supermarket goods.
- **Magnetic stripe cards** – used on bank and credit cards as well as on train and parking tickets.
- **Voice recognition** – still in its early stages because of difficulties with accents and data input speeds, but there are automated telephone systems that can respond to a limited range of voice inputs.
- **Biometrics** – measurements are taken of some physical feature of a person, such as the distance between points on the face. This can be used to authenticate people at airports.
- **RFID tags** (Radio Frequency Identification) – used to identify items in shops and are also useful on electronic travel tickets such as the London Oyster card.

Barcodes

4 902520 242716

Chip and Pin

BananaStock / Thinkstock

Magnetic Stripe Card

Quick Test

1. What is the measurement of facial features and their use in authenticating people called?
2. What is a check digit?
3. What is a range check?
4. What does validation do?

KEY WORDS

Make sure you understand these words before moving on!

- Form
- Drop-down box
- Validation
- Verification
- Range check
- Type check
- Check digit
- Biometrics
- RFID

Computer Control

Controlling Devices

The output from a computer doesn't have to be printed or on screen. Many important applications produce electronic signals as output. These signals can be used to control all sorts of devices.

For example…

- an autopilot
- the cruise control on a car
- a washing machine
- manufacturing on a production line.

Feedback

Many manufacturing processes are under computer control. For example, **sensors** can detect the temperature or composition of something that's being manufactured.

Sensors usually collect **analogue** data, but a computer needs **digital** data. So, the signals normally have to pass through an **analogue-to-digital converter** before a computer can use them.

The data is then fed into a computer system. The software checks the values against what they should be. Signals are then sent to **actuators** such as motors, heaters or relays to keep the values within limits.

This constant feeding back of sensor data and carrying out actions is called a **feedback loop**. A good example of this is in the control of the temperature in a greenhouse.

Controlling the Temperature in a Greenhouse

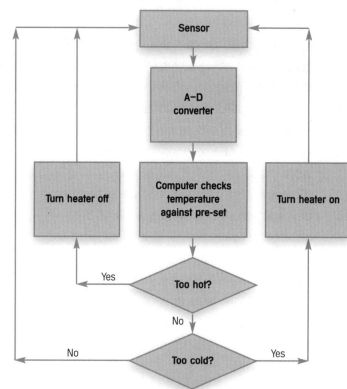

Robots

Robots are computer-controlled machines that carry out physical tasks for us.

Most robots are special purpose, like those which paint or weld cars on a production line.

Robots are often given their instructions by an embedded system rather than a general purpose computer.

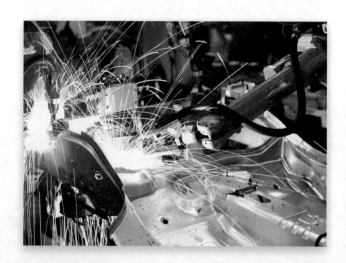

Control Programming

For a computer to control a situation, it must be given instructions. There are plenty of ways of doing this. One way is to use simple instructions to guide a robot around the floor.

The following are some instructions that draw a simple shape:	This is what the instructions mean:	If a robot is given these instructions, it will draw the shape below:
| ```
to shape
    home
    fd 50
    rt 90
    fd 50
    lt 90
    fd 50
    bk 100
end
``` | | 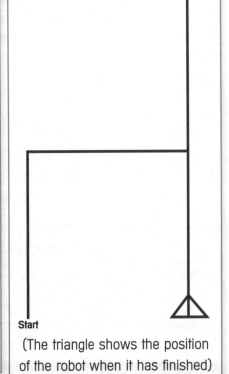<br>**Start**<br>(The triangle shows the position of the robot when it has finished) |

Command	Meaning
shape	The name of the procedure – the set of instructions
home	Sends the robot to the centre of the floor
fd	Forwards – you have to tell it how far to go
bk	Backwards – you have to tell it how far to go
rt	Right turn – you have to tell it the angle
lt	Left turn – you have to tell it the angle

Quick Test

1. What is a control program?
2. What sort of data does a sensor normally detect?
3. What is a feedback loop?
4. What is an actuator?

KEY WORDS

Make sure you understand these words before moving on!

- Sensor
- Analogue
- Digital
- Analogue-to-digital converter
- Actuator
- Feedback loop
- Robot
```

Data Logging

Data Logging

Computers can take their input from all sorts of devices. They use input from sensors in control applications. They can store and process data, which can help us carry out investigations.

Sensors take physical data and convert it to electrical signals. The electrical signals can then be converted into digital signals and fed into a computer.

There are sensors for every type of physical data. This makes it possible to record most events.

Physical Data Type	Example of Data Logging
Electrical	• Taxi meter • Traffic lights
Pressure	• Burglar alarm • Traffic census
pH	• Acidity of a chemical in manufacturing
Light	• Biometrics – authentication at airports, counting people
Magnetic	• Security door access control
Temperature	• Weather station

Data logging is particularly useful in scientific and environmental research. It can be used to detect earthquakes and warn of possible tsunamis.

Data logging can be combined with **GPS** technology to monitor the migrations of animals such as walruses. It can also monitor the changes in temperature and pressure in an explosion.

Advantages of data logging:
- More accurate than human data recording.
- Can monitor data 24/7.
- Can feed results straight into a computer system for processing or storage.
- Can collect data in difficult, dangerous or remote locations.

Disadvantages of data logging:
- Can be inflexible.
- Might miss new opportunities if the system is not programmed for them.

Telemetry and Visualisation

Telemetry is the use of telecommunications to transmit live data. Readings can easily be taken in remote or fast-moving locations and the results obtained immediately. In motor races, sensors on the cars transmit live data to the engineers about many things such as tyre temperatures, fuel, speed and gear changes.

The software that processes recorded data can display it in an easy-to-understand way. This is **visualisation**. The data can be used instantly to plot charts and create tables.

How Data is Logged

A sensor can be attached…

- to a data collection device that stores the data directly to a computer
- to a transmitter.

The data may be stored and processed later. The processing can be carried out using either a spreadsheet or special software.

Data is sampled at **intervals.** The choice of interval is important because enough data needs to be collected to make analysis meaningful.

Situation	Suitable interval
Cooling of a drink	1 min
Temperature changes in an explosion	1 millisecond
Climate change, e.g. temperatures	1 hour

Solar Weather Aerial

Quick Test

1. Why is data logging a better way to collect weather data compared with humans taking measurements?
2. Data logging is used to monitor the driving behaviour of a lorry driver. What would be a suitable sampling interval for this?
3. Give one situation where data logging temperature is used.
4. Give two types of sensor that could detect the passing of road traffic.

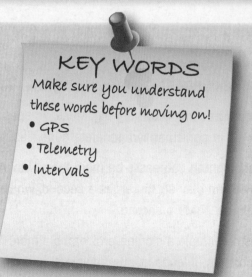

KEY WORDS
Make sure you understand these words before moving on!
- GPS
- Telemetry
- Intervals

Files and Compression

Files

Files are named stores of data on a computer backing store. Like all other computer data, they are streams of bits: 0s and 1s. They can represent any form of data, text, numbers, music, images, movies or instructions.

To make it easier for software and humans to interpret the data correctly, certain file types are recognised.

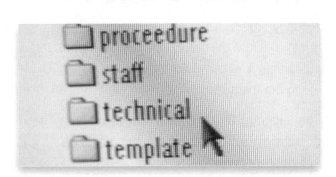

Structured and Unstructured Files

Some files have an organised structure. Databases are often arranged as a sequence of **records.** In a **relational** database, all the records have the same layout and size.

Most files are less structured. It's impossible to predict the sequence of bits in a picture, formatted word-processed document or program. Files like this are referred to as **binary files**.

Files are usually saved with an **extension**, which is an extra part of the file name that indicates the type of file that it is. The extension usually follows a dot in the file name.

Some extensions have become common, for example, the doc in 'letter.doc'. This indicates that the file is a word-processed document. It will be associated with the user's word processor.

The table below shows some common examples of different file types:

Extension	Description
doc	Word-processed file
xls	Excel spreadsheet
mdb	Microsoft database
pdf	Portable document format – this is used to save documents so they can be viewed exactly as they were created and it can be placed into many different applications.
HTM/HTML	A web page
MP3	A compressed sound format file
JPG/JPEG	A common compressed image file
ZIP	A general purpose compressed file or groups of files

Compression

Some files tend to be very big. Music, images and movies in particular can generate huge files.

A photograph can easily be more than 1Mb. A movie can play at 25 frames a second, which might be 25Mb a second.

This can create a storage problem, but more importantly, it leads to long download and upload times when sending them to another computer.

Compression is a way of making files take up less space. But, compressed files have to be decompressed when played back or displayed, which can lead to delays.

There are two main compression techniques:
* **Lossy** compression
* **Lossless** compression

Files and Compression

Lossy Compression

Some of the detail is taken out in **lossy compression** in order to make the file smaller. The idea is to remove data that matters the least. This means that you can't recover the original file when using this type of compression.

An **MP3** music file is only about a tenth the size of the original CD track. Data is removed that's considered beyond most people's perception, but some people say they can tell the difference.

JPEG images are lossy. You can control how much detail to lose.

Hemera / Thinkstock

Lossless Compression

Sometimes it's important to be able to restore the original material when decompressing a file. You can use **lossless compression** for this.

One way is to put words or other data into a dictionary with a code. Instead of storing the word many times, you store the code instead.

There are various algorithms for compressing without loss. Well-known examples are...
- LZW (Lempel-Ziv-Welch) algorithm
- ZIP files.

Uncompressed File

> **Ask not what your country can do for you, but what you can do for your country!** (Total: 79 bytes)

Compressed File

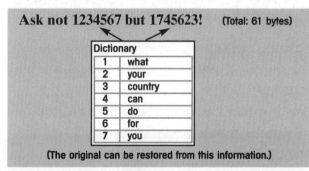

> **Ask not 1234567 but 1745623!** (Total: 61 bytes)

Dictionary	
1	what
2	your
3	country
4	can
5	do
6	for
7	you

(The original can be restored from this information.)

Quick Test

1. What is a file?
2. What is a file extension?
3. What is a binary file?
4. State one disadvantage of lossy compression.

KEY WORDS
Make sure you understand these words before moving on!
- File
- Record
- Binary file
- Extension
- Compression
- Lossy
- Lossless
- MP3

Security

Security Issues

Computers make it easy to store, transmit, copy and search for data.

This is a great opportunity for those who want to take advantage of other people's data for their own benefit. Data can also be lost by accident.

We have to be very careful to ensure that…
- valuable data doesn't fall into the wrong hands
- we don't accidentally lose data that's valuable to us.

Procedures should be put in place that reduce the risk of data loss or damage.

Backing Up

In case of disaster, we should always have **backups** of important data. Memory sticks and optical disks make it easy for everyone to make backups.

Organisations often use high volume tape storage.

Backups should be **stored** off-site in case of a serious problem. Online storage is one way to make sure there's a safe copy somewhere else.

How often a computer should be backed up

depends on how often the data changes. Backups should be carried out often enough so that the owner suffers no serious effects if data is lost.

Archiving is the storage of data that isn't in regular use anymore but might occasionally be needed. For example, a college might archive the details of students who left the previous year. After the data has been archived it can be deleted from the working system.

Network Security

Networks have special problems in terms of security. Many users need to have access, and it's important to let the right people look at the right data to get the jobs done. But, at the same time, data needs to be safe from unauthorised viewing and activity.

To ensure privacy, several methods of security can be put into place.

Levels of Access

Users are made members of groups. Different groups have different **privileges** so there's some information that not everyone is able to access.

User ID

A **user ID** says who you are and what groups you belong to. On a network, the network operating system looks up your user ID in a database to see what privileges you have.

Network Security (Cont.)

Passwords

Passwords are the key to security. Many people are careless with passwords. If **hackers** guess passwords they can gain access to confidential data.

Passwords should be:

- **Strong** (difficult to guess) – passwords should have a mixture of letters (upper and lower case), numbers and possibly symbols. They shouldn't be obvious, e.g. your birthday or favourite football team.
- **Long enough** – a short password is easier to crack.
- **Changed often** – in case someone learns them inadvertently.
- **Always kept secret** – some people simply reveal them when they are asked (hackers may pretend that they need them for maintenance). Some people write them on notices and stick them to the wall. Don't let anyone see you type in your password.

Physical

Data can be secured by keeping the server in a locked room. Access control systems require authorised users to authenticate themselves with a card, or by **biometrics**, before they can get into **data centres**.

Biometrics is using the measurement of some physical feature to identify a person. For example, facial features or fingerprints.

Data can be saved to two different servers at the same time so that if one has a disaster, there's another copy.

A UPS (uninterruptible power supply) makes sure that if the power goes down, there's a battery backup for a safe close down. Data being saved is not then lost.

And finally, sensible care should be taken when…

- disposing of old equipment with data on it
- carrying or sending data on disks or memory sticks.

Biometrics

Quick Test

1. What is meant by a strong password?
2. Why does the network operating system need to know your user ID?
3. What is archiving?
4. What is a UPS for?

KEY WORDS
Make sure you understand these words before moving on!
- Backing up
- Archiving
- Privileges
- User ID
- Password
- Hacker
- Strong
- Biometrics
- Data centre

Online Security

Hackers

Most computers are connected to the Internet at least some of the time. This means that hackers can attempt to gain access to your computer.

There are several reasons why someone might try to hack into your computer:

- To steal personal information – your credit card and bank details can be very useful to a thief.

- To use your computer to send **spam** – if a spammer takes control of thousands of PCs, stopping or deleting the culprit becomes harder.
- To send you advertising – your **browser** can be hijacked to look up favoured sites or to frighten you into thinking you have a virus.
- For fun – some hackers just have nothing better to do.

Online Threats

There are several different threats posed by being online.

Malware (malicious software)

Malware means any malicious software that's installed on your computer without you wanting it.

It includes a wide variety of types, which range from the annoying to the damaging.

Trojan horses

Trojan horses are run by the user, in the belief that they're something useful.

A Trojan horse is often picked up by a user from a website that looks harmless, but it installs malware when the site is accessed. For example, this may be in the form of **keyloggers,** which can send a record of your actions to a remote observer.

Wireless

Wireless can pose extra security problems because it's easy to intercept wireless signals.

Viruses

Viruses are programs that when run, make copies of themselves. They then use various methods such as email to spread to other computers.

Worms are viruses that spread through networks. Viruses and worms were once written as pranks but nowadays they're often the work of criminal gangs. Worms may carry a **payload**, which is designed to perform some action such as wiping data.

Data Transfer

Data is transmitted across most networks as a series of **packets.** In networks like the Internet, the packets are units of data that can be sent by different routes.

Packets can be intercepted on a network and analysed. This is even easier on a wireless network where you don't even have to be physically connected.

Precautions

There are several precautions that we can all take to protect our information from hackers.

Encryption

In case data does get intercepted, it's a good idea to **encrypt** it before sending it. This means scrambling it so that unauthorised people can't understand or read it. The person receiving the encrypted message needs to have a **key**, which is a special piece of information that allows the message to be decoded.

Firewalls

A **firewall** is either hardware or software that blocks unauthorised access to a computer system while allowing legitimate traffic.

One way that a firewall can work is to examine every packet that passes through and test it against certain rules that the user has set up. These rules might be based on where it has come from or where it's going.

Anti-malware

All computers connected to a network, especially the Internet, should have up-to-date software to scan incoming files and if necessary remove any malicious software.

Policies

Most organisations have rules about working online that help to protect information. For example...
* don't bring in removable media
* don't open attached programs
* don't visit certain types of web site, e.g. pornography or gambling.

All online activity may also be monitored.

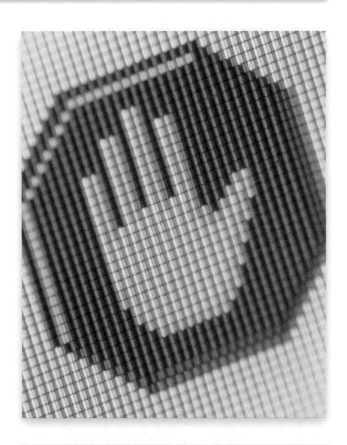

Quick Test

1. What is a computer virus?
2. What is a hardware or software solution used to block unauthorised access to a network?
3. What is a Trojan horse?
4. What is a keylogger?

KEY WORDS
Make sure you understand these words before moving on!
* Spam
* Browser
* Malware
* Trojan horse
* Keylogger
* Virus
* Worm
* Payload
* Packet
* Encryption
* Key
* Firewall

Practice Questions

1 What is the best software for writing a computer program? Tick the correct option.

A A word processor ◯   **B** An editor ◯

C A compiler ◯   **D** A spreadsheet ◯

2 Choose the correct words from the options given to complete the following sentences.

    hackers   **strong**   **numbers**   **privileges**   **ID**

A password needs to be _____ so that _____ can't easily guess it.

It should contain _____ as well as letters and should never be revealed to anybody.

The password is entered along with your _____ to give you the right

_____ in a network.

3 A cell in a spreadsheet contains =A12+B12. What is this? Tick the correct option.

A A formula ◯   **B** A function ◯

C A macro ◯   **D** A value ◯

4 Which of the following could be number fields in a database? Tick the **three** correct options.

A A telephone number ◯   **B** A postcode ◯   **C** A car registration ◯

D A person's height ◯   **E** A temperature ◯   **F** A test score ◯

5 Fill in the missing words to complete the following sentences.

An _____ is the boundary between the user and the _____ . If it's

easy to use, it's called _____ . You use a _____ to click on an

_____ in order to access the software that you want.

6 Which of these are automatic data capture methods? Tick the correct options.

A An on-screen form ◯   **B** OMR ◯   **C** Bar codes ◯

D A magnetic stripe ◯   **E** A drop-down box ◯   **F** A keyboard ◯

7 Circle the correct options in the following sentences.

a) A gender field in a database written as m or f is a **text / Boolean** field.

b) A sensor is an **input / output** device.

c) A named data store on a computer's hard disk is a **file / record**.

d) The storage of old data that is no longer required in daily use is called **backing up / archiving**.

e) A set of facts with no context is **information / data**.

8 Choose the correct words from the options given to complete the following sentences.

network	key	decrypt	encrypted	packets

Data transmitted across a _____ should be _____ so that anyone

intercepting the data _____ will not be able to understand it. The person it is being

sent to needs to have a _____ in order to _____ it.

9 What is the name of something in the real world about which we collect data? Tick the correct option.

A A record ◯   **B** A field ◯

C An entity ◯   **D** An attribute ◯

10 Fill in the missing words to complete the following sentences.

If a formula in a spreadsheet needs to be copied exactly, the cell references will have dollar signs added

so that they don't _____ when copied. This is called _____

_____ _____ . Another way to make sure that the reference

doesn't change is to give the data a _____ . We sometimes use a named

_____ to perform calculations, such as =SUM(A12:A20).

11 Match statements **A–E** to the correct type of data **1–5** in the table. Enter the appropriate numbers in the boxes provided.

1	Check digit	2	Bit-mapped	3	Vector graphic	4	Key field	5	Alphabetic

A A type of image file made up of many dots ◯

B An image file stored as mathematical relationships ◯

C A field in a database that can take only letters ◯

D A data item in a data table that uniquely identifies a record ◯

E An extra character added to a data item for validation purposes ◯

12 Explain why it's better to use automatic data capture when possible instead of manual data entry.

_____

_____

_____

The Internet

What is the Internet?

The **Internet** is a global network made up from smaller computer networks. It has transformed life for much of the world – about a quarter of the Earth's population uses it.

The networks are linked by cable, fibre optics and wireless systems. It's an infrastructure on which many services can be provided.

One of the most important reasons for the Internet's success is that it's standardised. It uses a common set of rules or **protocols** so that computers of all types can connect to it.

An **Internet Service Provider** (ISP) is a company that provides access to the Internet. An ISP also often provides other services, for example, email and data storage.

World Wide Web

It's important to realise that the **World Wide Web** is just one of the services carried on the Internet, although a very important one.

The 'web' is a collection of billions of web pages grouped on web sites. These pages are all based on the **HTML** (Hypertext Markup Language) standard page description language.

This language is understood by browsers that can produce screen displays according to the codes embedded in a page. The pages are transmitted using **HTTP** (**Hypertext Transfer Protocol**).

Hypertext is text with embedded links. When you click on the links, you get taken to a different location.

HTML is a system of '**tags**' in angle brackets (**‹›**). They tell the browser how to display text or what to do. For example, **‹h1›** means that what follows is a top level header and must be displayed in large letters.

HTML Code

```
<html>
<body>
 <h1>Get the best results with
Lonsdale Revision Books</h1>
<p>Quality Revision Guides</p>
<IMG
SRC="html%20example_html_m8503e45.j
pg" NAME="graphics1" ALIGN=LEFT
WIDTH=267 HEIGHT=377 BORDER=0><BR
CLEAR=LEFT><BR>
</P>
</body>
</html>
```

When HTML code is read by a browser, it displays it as instructed.

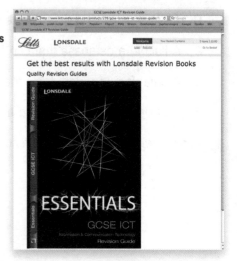

Search Engines

With so much information on so many websites, finding what you need can be difficult. We use **search engines** to help us. These are web sites that hold databases about other web sites.

Search engines provide software that can catalogue websites and respond to our requests. Commercial search engines make their money by providing advertising services.

Many enquiries generate millions of 'hits', which means that many web sites are so low down on the list that they never get looked at.

The most popular search engine, Google, has a system called Page Rank that ranks pages according to the number of links that there are to them.

Companies can also get a higher ranking for their web sites by paying the search engine provider.

Other Services from Search Engines

Some search engines have expanded their scope to include other useful services, for example:

- **Google Earth** lets you see anywhere on the planet either from space or on a map. In many places there's a street view too. This concerns some people as they don't want their movements monitored.
- Some search engines provide **directions** from one place to another.
- A **translation** option is often given where you translate between most languages, although the results aren't always very good.
- Many search engines provide chat, email and photo sharing facilities.

Quick Test

1. What is an ISP?
2. What is the difference between the Internet and the World Wide Web?
3. What is hypertext?
4. How do commercial search engines make their money?

KEY WORDS

Make sure you understand these words before moving on!

- Internet
- Protocols
- Internet Service Provider
- World Wide Web
- HTML
- Hypertext Transfer Protocol
- Hypertext
- Tags
- Search engines

Online Safety

New Dangers

The Internet presents dangers as well as benefits. We have to learn a new set of safety precautions so that we get the best out of this world of information and communication without getting into trouble.

It is important to remember that anything you put on a web site may be seen by people who should not see it. There is no such thing as total privacy on the Internet.

Chat

We can have instant conversations with anyone else, anywhere in the world. These 'chats' can be with a **webcam** and voice as well as text.

When chatting online, it's easy to pretend to be someone else. You should never give out personal details to someone you don't know. It's the same as in real life, but online you often get a false sense of security.

You should also be careful about sending pictures of yourself. If you don't know the person well you don't know what they might do with your pictures. For example, would you like the pictures posted on web sites for everyone to see?

You should be wary about meeting someone in person who you have only met online. Never meet someone new except in a public place, and never meet them alone.

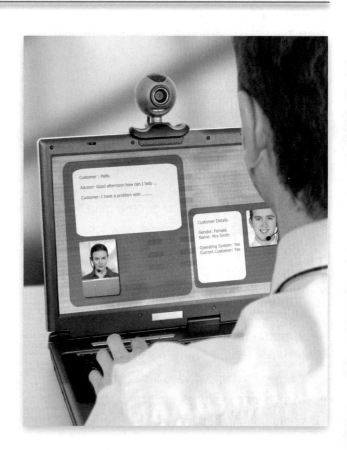

Social Networking Sites

Lots of people put enormous amounts of detail about themselves on **social networking** sites such as Facebook and Bebo.

Apart from criminals using such information, it's routine for companies to check out Facebook profiles when shortlisting job applicants.

So, be careful what information you include. For example, if you admit to some youthful indiscretion or post pictures of yourself in a compromising situation you may be passed over for the job or even lose your existing job.

Remember too that the police and other government agencies regularly look at publicly available details. How much surveillance do you want in your life?

If you do use social networking sites, then you should make sure that you use the privacy settings, which allow you to control who can view your personal information.

Phishing and Other Scams

Phishing is an attempt to obtain sensitive details from you, e.g. bank information or personal details, which could be used for **identity theft.** With enough of someone's personal details, it's possible to open a bank or credit card account.

For example, look at the email opposite.

This may at first glance look tempting, but think about the following:
- Would an official draw be signed by someone with a yahoo address?
- Why do they need so much detail about you?
- Notice the spelling mistakes.
- Notice the grammatical mistakes.

The Internet provides many opportunities for scammers. Look for bad English, requests for personal details, unbelievable return addresses, etc.

Remember that a bank will never ask for a password from you (contact your own bank if you are in doubt).

Some phishing emails have official-looking logos on them, but then have links to the criminals' web site.

Maybe it's a good thing that the Internet makes us more suspicious and careful.

Example of Identity Theft Email

E-mail

Delete | Reply ▾ | Forward | Spam

International Promotion / Prize Award Dept.
From: Microware Corporation Email Lottery International
World Internet Lotto Center
Western Avenue 4712

Dear Winner,

We are pleased to inform you of the final announcement of The Sponsored lotto Online Promo Program held by MICROWARE CORPORATION.

The draw were done electronically with several email addresses provided to this office by web mail providers to enhance the utilization of the internet.

Your email addres was attached to:
Serial number 789-376
Ticket Number: 675452891033/397
Lucky numbers: 5-0-15-42-1-679

To file for your claims and due remittance of funds contact:
Mr. James Galloway
Address: Microware Ltd.UK
Elm House, 76 Buckingham Palace Road
London/United Kingdom.
E-mail: jamie-xavier.galloway@yahoo.net
Phone: +44-7601-5814-70

with your information which includes:
Your full names:
Your full home / office address:
Nationality:
Direct Land/Mobile phone/fax numbers:
Occupation / Age:
Sex:
Next of kin:

Yours Sincerely,
Mrs. Miranda Cliff
(Promotion co-coordinator)

Delete | Reply ▾ | Forward | Spam

Quick Test

1. Give two precautions you should take when you have met someone online.
2. Why do companies check out social networking sites?
3. What is phishing?
4. What is identity theft?

KEY WORDS
Make sure you understand these words before moving on!
- Webcam
- Social networks
- Phishing
- Identity theft

Online Services

Shopping

The Internet has changed the way we shop.

Some people still prefer the social experience of physical shopping, but many others get a lot of their shopping online, from groceries and clothes to insurance and holidays.

Online **auction sites** make selling as easy as buying.

It's easy to find reviews of vendors and services, so we can see what experiences other people have had.

Advantages:
- Far more choice than shopping centres and we can buy from anywhere, whenever we want.
- You can hunt around for the best deals or even find web sites that do that for you.

Disadvantages:
- You can't always be sure that you will like what you see online.
- There are security issues with payment.
- You have to trust the vendor to deliver.

Banking

You can conduct all your banking needs online.

You can set up and cancel payments, look at your statements and transfer money between accounts.

Online banking means writing fewer cheques and there is no need to have statements sent to you by post. You can see the state of your accounts at any time so it's easier to avoid getting overdrawn.

Advantages:
- 24/7 access.
- It's easy to keep on top of your finances.
- There's no need to go to the bank.

Disadvantages:
- Possibility of fraud.
- Possibility of snooping on spending behaviour.

News and Resources

There are resources for everything online, though some have to be paid for. For example:
- You can buy pictures for publications for a small fee.
- Professionals can join groups for a fee so that they have access to the latest knowledge about their work.
- Examining bodies have all the details about their qualifications as well as training courses for teachers.

One of the most well-known sources of information is Wikipedia, where volunteers write material on all subjects for no charge. Other free resources come from publishers of encyclopaedias and other books. You can look up any computer term in webopedia.

Advantages:
- You can find information on almost any subject very quickly.
- Information can be up-to-the minute, e.g. if there's a plane crash, it will be online in minutes.
- You can read news reports from all over the world and learn languages at the same time.

Disadvantages:
- There is no guarantee that the information is reliable – you have to be careful that the writers of materials know their subject and aren't just trying to put across a point of view.

Language Translators

Some sites can translate text.

Advantages:

- They can help when you are learning a new language.

Disadvantages:

- Translation is not something that can be mechanised very well. You often get some very strange results!
- Human languages can be complicated and unpredictable, and human experience and judgment is needed to do this well.

Instructional Packages

There is so much information avaliable on the web that you can learn practically anything online.

For example…

- tutorials for software packages
- you can sign up to courses – some of them free
- you can learn a language, e.g. one site combines a chat/social networking site with a language learning theme.

Your own school or college might put learning content online using a **Virtual Learning Environment (VLE)**.

Your teachers can also set and mark work online.

Advantages:

- You can learn at any time at any place.
- You can have access to native language speakers.

Disadvantages:

- It can be hard to motivate yourself when learning on your own.
- The quality of online learning materials may not always be high.
- Lack of feedback can hold back learning.

Quick Test

1. Give one advantage of banking online.
2. What is a VLE?
3. Why are online translators often not very reliable?
4. Give one reason why someone might go online to catch up with the news.

KEY WORDS

Make sure you understand these words before moving on!
- Auction site
- Virtual Learning Environment

Communications

Personal Communications

The Internet has transformed the way we communicate. We probably communicate more than we used to, but in a different way.

We write fewer letters and now expect our communication to be instant in many cases. We expect to be contactable more.

Email

Email is the preferred method of communication for many purposes, especially in business. It's fast and convenient. We don't need to hang on the phone while someone is found, or wait for a letter to be sent in the post.

Email comes in two main forms – **client based** and **web based**:

- Client based – most businesses install an **email client** such as Outlook™ on their staff computers. This allows the sending of large files and integration into other scheduling and planning features.
- Web based – many search engine companies and others provide **webmail,** which is email that can be accessed by a browser from anywhere. Limits on file sizes are often imposed.

Any email service will provide certain standard services, for example…

- forwarding
- file **attachments**
- file organisation
- **cc** (carbon copy)
- address books
- **encryption**
- **digital signatures** (an encrypted message that verifies who has sent the email).

Other Communication Methods

VoIP

VoIP (Voice over Internet Protocol) is a way of using the Internet to make voice conversations. The difference between VoIP and using the telephone is that…

- the transmission is digital
- it's sent via packet switching
- it's usually free (even internationally)
- it requires the parties to be online at the same time
- it needs broadband access
- it often allows visual contact as well as voice.

Online Chat

Online chat is generally a one-on-one, instant conversation over the Internet, although others can join in if invited. It evolved from the use of terminals to communicate with servers in mainframe operation.

It can be used in business meetings as well as for leisure. Online conferences often have a chat facility built in.

Other Communication Methods (Cont.)

Blogs

Many people like to keep online diaries called **Blogs** (short for weblogs) and invite comments. Some of these get noticed and achieve fame or notoriety. Blogs can be used to great effect, sometimes to challenge governments and others.

Microblogs are an abbreviated form of blogging where you post your thoughts in a few words. They can sometimes produce dramatic effects such as when describing the events in the Iranian elections.

Social networking

Many people use **social networking** sites to keep in touch with old friends and to make new ones. They are good places to share photos and experiences.

But, they are also dangerous places if you put too much information about yourself on show. You need to make sure that your **privacy settings** keep you safe.

Social networking sites can be addictive. Many people spend more time on these sites than they do interacting in real life.

Impact on Society

The impacts of Internet communications are developing all the time.

We can all check out a hotel or an airline before we book by looking at reviews by real users.

Big organisations can be seriously affected by individuals (or the 'little people') if they use a bit of ingenuity.

For example, a passenger of a large airline had his guitar damaged by the baggage handlers. The airline wouldn't deal with the complaint properly so he sang a song about it and posted it on YouTube. It went **viral** – in other words it got passed around millions of people. The airline's share value dropped $180 million as a result of the bad publicity.

Quick Test

1. What is a microblog?
2. State one advantage of webmail over client based email.
3. State one disadvantage of using VoIP.
4. State one disadvantage of using social networking sites.

KEY WORDS

Make sure you understand these words before moving on!
- Email client
- Webmail
- Attachment
- Cc
- Encryption
- Digital signature
- VoIP
- Online chat
- Blog
- Microblog
- Social networking
- Privacy settings
- Viral

Entertainment

Video Hosting

IT has had a big impact on entertainment just as it has on every other aspect of life.

Lots of web sites now offer the possibility of **video hosting** (showing videos taken by users). This has been made even easier because it's possible to make videos not only with video cameras but also with web cams, digital cameras and phones. Also, clips of shows and other entertainment can be uploaded. This has opened up the world of video making and publishing to all.

Advantages:
- It helps the sales of live concert tickets as well as recorded videos and music.
- Shots of news events can be posted so that interesting events are available to view.
- It's another way to communicate your ideas.

Disadvantages:
- These sites are often abused by posting criminal or undesirable activities.
- Many postings are just boring or badly made.

Bookings

It's easy to make bookings online.

For example, if you want to book seats at a theatre, you can go online and see the seats that are available. You can also sometimes see a view of the stage from the seat.

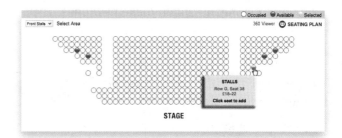

Radio and Video Streaming

You can download media files and play them on a PC or MP3 player. Alternatively, if you have enough **bandwidth** and processing power, you can **stream** music, radio and television onto a PC.

Streaming means that the data is run into a **buffer,** which then feeds its content to the processor for decoding and playing. It involves huge amounts of data and needs a powerful processor.

The increasing commercialisation of the Internet has driven many of these advances.

These services are not free – you need to pay for bandwidth – and the files still have to be compressed, losing some quality and slowing down playback.

Broadcasters offer many of their TV programmes as streaming video.

Music Downloads

For many years people used to share music files using **peer-to-peer** techniques. This avoided using servers on the Internet and involved **illegal copyright** violations. This file sharing led to a reduction in sales of CDs.

Legal action has reduced this sharing and there are now sites that charge very little for a **legal download,** which you can store on your PC or MP3 player. Software is often offered to make it easy to organise and move your files between devices.

Gaming

Computer games are big business. With the development of **Java** and **Flash** the quality has improved and the games are more exciting.

Online Games

Online games sometimes involve huge numbers of players and are then called **massively multiplayer online role-playing games** (**MMORPG**). With many online games you create an online person (**avatar**) to represent you.

Stand-alone Computer Games

Games are available to play on a PC or a games console. Games consoles are among the most powerful personal computers available in the general market with particularly impressive graphics processing.

Online Gambling

Many companies offer the opportunity to play poker, blackjack, roulette and other games to gamblers. As with many other businesses, there are now many bookmakers online, meaning it's now possible to bet on horse racing online.

Because it's easy to remain anonymous online, some people gamble who might not otherwise do so because they would be nervous about using a real casino or bookmaker.

Jupiterimages / Thinkstock

Quick Test

1. What is a buffer?
2. Give one advantage of booking a theatre seat online compared with going to the box office.
3. Why is a games console fitted with more powerful graphics processing than a PC?
4. What is video streaming?

KEY WORDS

Make sure you understand these words before moving on!

- Video hosting
- Bandwidth
- Streaming
- Buffer
- Peer-to-peer
- Copyright
- Download
- Java
- Flash
- MMORPG
- Avatar

Legal Matters

Computer Crime

Computers are now very often used in crime. **Computer forensics** is a rapidly developing aspect of IT and concentrates on finding evidence of crimes in computer systems.

Most computer crime relates to unauthorised access to systems. This can be followed by espionage, theft or other misuse of data.

Types of Computer Crime

Hacking

Hacking is unauthorised access to a system. Hackers generally try to obtain or bypass security mechanisms, either by guessing passwords, asking for them (some people will give them away without realising!) or using brute force techniques where software tries millions of different passwords.

Copyright

It's now very easy to copy digital resources, so infringement of copyright on intellectual property such as software, books, films and music is a common crime.

Some people don't regard it as particularly serious but if creative people don't get rewarded for their efforts it becomes pointless for them to continue to produce new work.

Spam

Spam is unsolicited email, mostly advertising. It's one of the curses of the information age. Spam…
- wastes time and bandwidth
- clogs servers
- costs money to filter / remove.

Spam filters can block the worst of it but the best defence is never to respond to it.

Harassment

With the growth of social networking, cyber harassment is getting more common, (cyber harassment is bullying through the Internet, e.g. via Facebook.)

Stalking is possible on such sites too, by intruding excessively into social interactions.

Confidentiality

Personal data is protected in most countries, but selling and copying information is commonplace. There have also been recent cases where the UK government has lost personal data (e.g. disks containing sensitive personal information have been lost in the postal system).

Fraud

Once a hacker gets into a computer system, there are plenty of ways in which he or she can profit from it:
- Data can be altered.
- New data can be added.
- Illegal transactions can be concealed.
- Identities can be stolen.
- Money can be transferred.
- Confidential data, such as trade secrets, can be copied or sold.

WARNING

IDENTITY THEFT DETECTED

You are requested to take action immediately

Laws

The **Data Protection Act** 1998 is a typical law designed to protect people's privacy when their personal data is stored on a computer system. It's a UK law but most countries have something similar.

The Act requires data controllers (those who hold such data) to register with a government agent called the Information Commissioner.

A person whose details are held by a data controller is called a data subject. There are some exemptions from the Act, for example, the police and security agencies do not need to disclose the data that they hold. Also, recent UK laws allow many public bodies to access people's phone and internet records. This was originally intended to combat terrorism but it is increasingly being misused for other purposes.

The Act has the following principles:
- Data may only be used for the specific purposes for which it was collected.
- Data must be accurate.
- Data mustn't be disclosed to other parties without the consent of the individual.
- Individuals can access the information held about them.
- Personal information may be kept for no longer than is necessary and must be kept up to date.
- Personal information may not be sent outside the European Union.
- Adequate security measures must be in place to protect personal data.

The UK **Computer Misuse Act** 1990 was an attempt to criminalise hacking.

Quick Test

1. Who is targeted by the UK Computer Misuse Act?
2. Give two examples of what may be regarded as intellectual property.
3. What is spam?
4. What is the main concern of computer forensics?

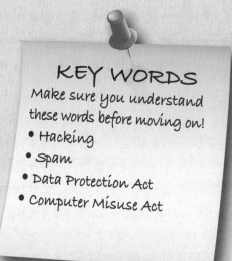

KEY WORDS
Make sure you understand these words before moving on!
- Hacking
- Spam
- Data Protection Act
- Computer Misuse Act

Social Issues

Disability and Visual Impairment

Computers have brought such benefits to so many people that we sometimes forget that they aren't accessible to everyone.

Using a PC can be a problem for some people. To use a PC as it 'comes out of the box' you need normal eyesight, reasonable hearing and flexible fingers to use the keyboard and mouse, but...

- if you break an arm you may not be able to type properly.
- some people have weak sight, are colour blind or totally blind.

There are various ways that disabled people can be helped to use a computer.

For people who can't see well, it's possible to enlarge the text or have the computer speak its output using a **speech synthesiser.** The screen colours can be changed and the **icons** enlarged. Special printers can produce **Braille** output.

You can get software that takes voice input. It has to be programmed to recognise a particular voice because voices vary so much.

Keyboard and Mouse Options

Sticky keys are useful if you only have the use of one hand. You can press the shift key (or control or Alt key) and it remains effective until you have pressed the letter you want.

The mouse cursor can be controlled from the numeric keypad if you find the mouse difficult to use.

Access to Computers and Internet

Not everyone has access to a computer or the Internet.

In an industrialised country this is usually a matter of choice, although broadband provision in the UK is patchy. Not being able to access the Internet can cut people off from some very useful services and information.

However, worldwide connection to the Internet is variable. Some countries have virtually no broadband, whereas others, such as South Korea, have ultra fast connections of up to 1Gbps commonly available.

Health and Safety

There are some common dangers associated with using computers, especially for people who use them a lot:

- **RSI (Repetitive Strain Injury)** – excessive use of a keyboard or mouse can cause tendon damage and pain. Wrist ache is often the result.
- **Eye strain** – staring closely at a screen can cause visual problems. This is made worse if there is back lighting or flicker to the screen.
- **Neck ache** – a bad posture can result in neck and back problems. It's important to use a good **ergonomically** designed office chair and adjust it to your needs if using a computer extensively.
- **General comfort** – computer rooms can get very hot, especially in summer. This can lead to dehydration and headaches.

The following advice will help you to work safely and comfortably at a computer:

- Take frequent breaks.
- Have suitable lighting.
- Make sure cables aren't tripping hazards.
- Adjust chairs correctly.
- Have the screen at a comfortable height.
- Use air conditioning to keep temperatures comfortable.
- Don't eat or drink at the keyboard.
- Have regular eye examinations.

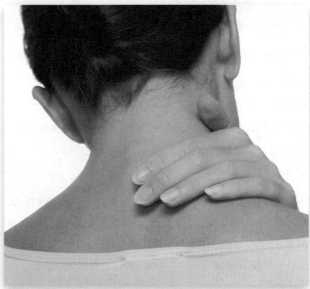

Quick Test

1. How can a colour-blind person make it easier for them to use a PC?
2. What do you have to do before speech recognition software will understand you?
3. What are sticky keys?
4. How can you avoid neck ache when using a computer a lot?

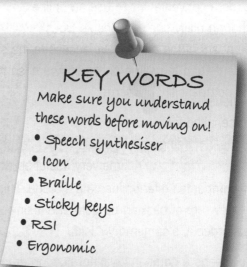

KEY WORDS
Make sure you understand these words before moving on!
- Speech synthesiser
- Icon
- Braille
- Sticky keys
- RSI
- Ergonomic

Modern Work Issues

Impact of IT on Work

Most aspects of work have been affected by developments in IT. For example:

- Managers are more likely to produce their own documents rather than send them to a secretary.
- People work on the move, on trains and planes.
- Information is available almost everywhere.
- People can be contacted almost anywhere, 24/7.

There are advantages and disadvantages to this, but at least there are more choices available as to how we work.

Collaborative Working

IT makes it easy for lots of people to work together.

Video conferencing allows groups to have discussions anywhere, even on the other side of the world. People can share documents and have voice and visual communication. VoIP makes this available to everyone.

Several people can work on the same document by emailing it around. If 'track changes' is used then all alterations are visible so it's easy to see who has suggested what.

Even more convenient is to use an online file-sharing utility such as Google Docs™. With that, all members of the group have access to the same documents and the same online software, so there are no compatibility problems.

Data Storage

Many companies offer online data storage. This can save the worry of backing up data and losing portable media, e.g. memory sticks.

It also means a company will not need to employ experts in data storage.

Software as a Service

One development of the online storage idea is being able to sign up to a company that offers **Software as a Service** (SaaS).

A wide variety of specialist software is available this way, such as help desk applications. You license the software and can use it online whenever you want.

Advantages of SaaS:
- There's no need to buy software.
- Software is updated as part of the service.
- You don't need a lot of infrastructure to store your software.
- Data is stored safely and there's no need to pay for your own security systems.
- The vendor has a reliable source of income from the licensing.
- There's a tendency for more standardisation, making it easier for businesses to share information.
- The software is usually adaptable to suit a particular business.
- The business gets to see good practice developed with the help of other users.

Disadvantages of SaaS:
- There's loss of control over data storage.
- There's less control over software upgrades.

Developments such as these are sometimes called **cloud computing**. The Internet is often represented as a cloud in diagrams. The client isn't concerned with technical details but just sends the data somewhere where everything is taken care of.

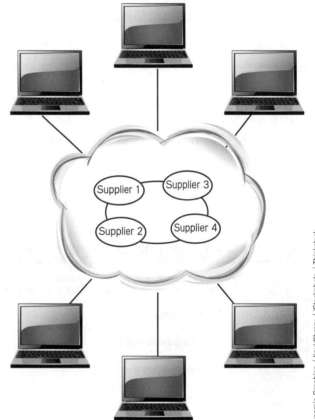

Dynamic Graphics / liquidlibrary / iStockphoto / Thinkstock

Quick Test

1. What does 'track changes' mean?
2. State one advantage of using online storage for a company.
3. What is Software as a Service?
4. State one disadvantage of using Software as a Service.

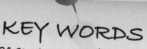

KEY WORDS
Make sure you understand these words before moving on!
- Video conferencing
- Software as a Service
- Cloud computing

Working with IT Systems

Getting the Best from PCs

Modern PCs are designed to be easy to use. Nearly everything is automated. It's good because most actions are **intuitive**, in other words the computer behaves as you think it will. The downside is that the computer sometimes makes decisions for you that you don't want.

Software usually comes with lots of **default settings** (settings that you get if you don't change anything), which may not suit you. So, there is still work to be done to get the best out of any system.

Starting Up and Shutting Down

Once you have switched the computer on, the operating system will load (**boot**) from the hard disk.

Most systems these days allow different users to have their own **profiles.** You can set this up so that each user has an individual desk top with individual browser settings and **history.**

Ideally, you should password-protect your login.

There are many things that you might want to change about your user profile, such as the browser you prefer to use. There are **utilities** that let you set your **user preferences.**

It's important to **shut down** properly. Various files need to be updated to make sure that your next session starts the way you want it.

So, select the shut down option and don't just switch off.

Customising a PC

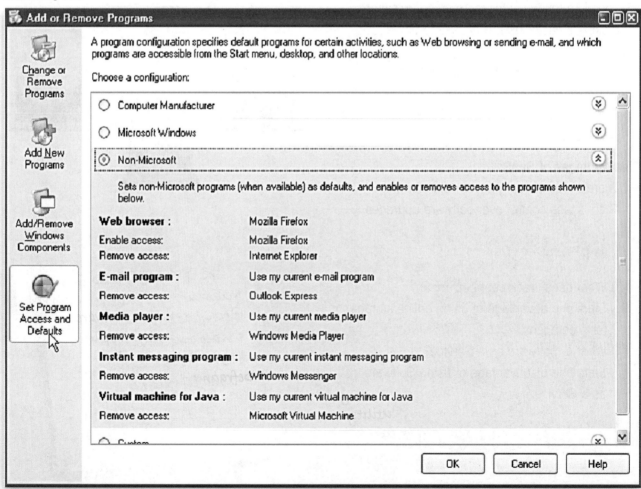

Maintenance

It doesn't take long to accumulate lots of files. You can make life easier for yourself by organising them into logical **folders** (directories).

Give the folders and files meaningful names, i.e. choose names that will remind you of exactly what they are for.

Peripherals such as printers need looking after. Replacing ink cartridges in an ink jet printer is sometimes more expensive than buying a new printer. In order to reduce your printing costs...

* make use of print preview
* consider getting a cheap laser printer
* load the paper carefully to avoid paper jams.

Running the Computer

Most computers slow down with age, often due to **fragmentation**. This means that the files get split across the hard disk so that loading them takes many disk accesses instead of just one. You should run the **defragment** utility from time to time to consolidate the files.

Another thing that slows the computer down is running unnecessary software. Some virus protection programs cause long delays by scanning everything. So, choose an efficient **virus scanner** and make sure that it updates itself when you want it to, not when it decides.

Using the Internet puts huge numbers of history and **cache** files on your hard disk.

Many websites put **cookies** on your hard disk. Cookies are small text files that store information about your actions on a web site.

Get a CleanUp Utility to free up disk space. You should also clean up your hard disk from time to time as you may not want other people looking at what you have been doing.

Protection

If you connect to the Internet, you should have protection against malware. Installing a good protection suite should be a top priority.

Run an anti-**adware** utility from time to time to stop any unwanted **pop-ups** and clear out files that threaten your privacy. This also frees up a lot of disk space.

Quick Test

1. What does booting mean?
2. Why do PCs slow down with age?
3. Why is it a good idea to have different logins on a shared PC?
4. Why is it a good idea to run adware protection software?

KEY WORDS

Make sure you understand these words before moving on!

* Intuitive
* Default settings
* Boot
* Profile
* History
* Utility
* User preference
* Folder
* Peripheral
* Fragmentation
* Defragment
* Virus scanner
* Cache
* Cookie
* Adware
* Pop-up

Practice Questions

1 What is the name of a small text file placed on a PC by a web site? Tick the correct option.

A A virus ◯   **B** A cache file ◯   **C** A cookie ◯   **D** A hyperlink ◯

2 Which of the following is a way of communicating by voice over the Internet? Tick the correct option.

A WAP ◯   **B** Bluetooth ◯   **C** VoIP ◯   **D** WiFi ◯

3 Choose the correct words from the options given to complete the following sentences.

phishing   **privacy**   **identity**   **photos**   **spam**   **theft**   **friends**

Social networking sites are a good place to share _____ but you have to be careful

not to reveal too much about yourself. You need to set your _____ settings so that only

your _____ can see your personal details. Sometimes you will get

_____ which tries to persuade you to give away bank details. This is known as

_____ and can lead to _____ _____ .

4 Which of the following is good advice for making a computer more comfortable to use? Tick the **three** correct options.

A Have a window behind the screen ◯

B Use bright background colours ◯

C Use an ergonomically-designed chair ◯

D Take frequent breaks ◯

E Have the screen at the correct angle ◯

F Keep the room as warm as possible ◯

5 Fill in the missing words to complete the following sentences.

A PC may start to run slowly after a while. This can be caused by _____ where files

get split over the _____ . You can fix this problem by running

_____ software, which is a _____ . Some _____

checkers also slow down the computer while they scan for infections.

6 By what method can people share files online without going through a server? Tick the correct option.

A Peer-to-peer connections ◯

B Streaming ◯

C An ISP ◯

D POP ◯

7 Circle the correct options in the following sentences.

a) A law to protect personal data on computer systems is the **Data Protection Act / Computer Misuse Act.**

b) Accessing software and services online is known as **Cloud Computing / Software licensing**.

c) An online diary is known as a **blog / chat room**.

d) Music streamed into a PC goes through a **buffer / disk** before being played.

e) Text on a web site with links to other places is called **HTML / hypertext**.

8 Choose the correct words from the options given to complete the following sentences.

synthesiser   sticky   braille   voice   keys   speech

Blind people can read output from a computer if it's printed in _____ . They can also

make use of a _____ so that they can listen to the output.

_____ input is useful for someone with a broken arm and _____

_____ can help that person use the shift key.

9 Explain why a company might want to make use of Software as a Service instead of buying its own software licenses.

_____

_____

_____

_____

_____

_____

Answers

Quick Test Answers

Page 5
1. A collection of items controlled by a computer.
2. **Any one of: Advantages:** Small size; Light; Web access
   Disadvantages: Small keyboard; Small screen
3. **Accept any suitable examples:** Washing machine; Microwave oven; Satellite receiver; Phone; Camera
4. One that's designed for one particular job.

Page 7
1. RAM
2. The processor
3. 5 x 1024 x 1024 x 1024 = 5368709120 bytes
4. A bit

Page 9
1. Digital signals
2. **Accept any suitable example:** Reduce errors; Reduce costs; Faster input
3. **Accept any suitable example:** Lottery ticket; Exam answers
4. **Accept any suitable example:** Keypad; Touch screen; Card reader

Page 11
1. **Accept any suitable answer:** Legal proof; To read away from a computer; For a permanent record
2. **Accept any suitable example:** Less power used; Runs cold; Lasts longer; Smaller footprint
3. Dot matrix printer
4. **Accept any suitable example:** Architect; Designer; Engineer

Page 13
1. Bit   2. 1 byte   3. Pixels   4. RAM

Page 15
1. The USB stick is easily lost. 2. A laser 3. Magnetic 4. The hard disk

Page 19
1. **Accept any suitable example:** Obstruction; Mountains; Tunnels; Out of sight of a base station

2. **Accept any suitable example:** MP3; Windows Media Audio
3. 3
4. A protocol
5. Broadband
6. Media Access Control – a unique number assigned to a network card.

Page 21
1. NIC (Network Interface Card)
2. **Accept any suitable example:** Flexible; Easy to add new nodes; No building work.
3. Login ID and password
4. Hub or switch.

Page 23
1. LAN
2. A computer that provides services to other computers.
3. The whole network goes down.
4. Peer-to-peer

Answers to Practice Questions
Pages 24–25
1. D
2. A
3. characters / letters; Unicode; pixels; bit-mapped
4. A, B
5. **a)** broadband **b)** 1KB **c)** ROM **d)** WiFi
6. B
7. hotspot; encrypted; WEP; WP2; SSID
8. sat nav; 3; triangulation, database; software; speech synthesiser
9. operating system; hard disk / backing storage; RAM / memory; processor / control unit
10. B, D
11. A5, B2, C4, D3, E1
12. High bandwidth is needed for fast downloads. Some files, e.g. music files are very large and it would take a long time to download them without a high bandwidth.

Quick Test Answers

Page 27
1. A set of instructions given to a computer.
2. An operating system
3. A defragmenter
4. Software to do a particular real-world job

Page 29
1. Device driver
2. False, they just appear to.
3. When the response from an input is immediate.
4. When the data or programs are collected together then run without further intervention.

Page 31
1. A named data store on a computer storage device.
2. A grouping of files / directory.
3. A storage system where directories exist in other directories.
4. Extra letters on the end of a file name that indicate the type of file that it is.

Page 33
1. A picture used to represent an action or object on screen.
2. Mouse / other pointing device.
3. A control
4. Dialogue box

Page 35
1. IS manager
2. Analyst

3. **Accept any suitable example:** Logging problems; Deciding priorities; Arranging solutions
4. Technicians

Page 37
1. Feasibility Study
2. To demonstrate faults and to ensure it's fit for purpose.
3. Implementing a new system while continuing to run the old one.
4. Making changes after implementation.

Answers to Practice Questions
Pages 38–39
1. B
2. B
3. open source; free; source code; proprietary; Windows; Microsoft
4. A, B, C
5. **a)** utility
   b) processor
   c) GUI
   d) operations manager
   e) help desk team
6. file; folder; extension; word processor; web page
7. D
8. spreadsheet; inexpensive; users; bugs; testing
9. A, D, E
10. interface; computer; intuitive; mouse; icon
11. It may have bugs in it, the user's requirements might change, it may be improved, new features may be required.

Manipulating Data

Quick Test Answers

Page 41
1. Facts **2.** Context **3.** An internet news page. **4.** By scanning the bar code

Page 43
1. Text editor or web authoring software.
2. The option that you get if you don't change any of the settings.
3. Template
4. Marks / highlights any changes that you make.

Page 45
1. Footer **2.** Select print preview **3.** Macro **4.** House style

Page 47
1. Morphing
2. A dot that makes up a picture.
3. As a mathematical expression.
4. An image made out of a very large number of dots, which create a clear image.

Page 49
1. Uniform Resource Locator – the address of a web resource.
2. Click the back button.
3. It gives one-click access to a function.
4. If you had clicked on the wrong page or if a page was very slow to upload.

Page 53
1. A function
2. A range
3. A sign that causes an action to be carried out.
4. Find the largest number in the range (A1:A12).
5. The A1 would adjust, but the B1 would not.
6. As a number
7. Chart / graph; Pivot table
8. A mathematical representation of reality.

Page 55
1. A special effect when changing from one slide to the next.
2. A presentation made of more than two of: text, graphics, movies, animations and sounds.
3. Use a master slide
4. Template

Page 57
1. DBMS – Database Management System
2. A unique field that identifies a record.
3. A real world object for which we store data.
4. A database divided into linked tables.

Page 59
1. AND **2.** Boolean **3.** Text / string / alphanumeric **4.** Integer

Page 61
1. Biometrics
2. An extra digit produced by a calculation and added to a number to check that it's input correctly.
3. A check that a value falls between two extreme values.
4. Checks that data input is acceptable.

Page 63
1. A computer program designed to control some physical device or system.
2. Analogue
3. Collecting data from a situation and acting on it.
4. A device that carries out a physical action, possibly under computer control.

Page 65
1. More reliable / accurate, more readings can be taken, easy to store / process data.
2. Every second – no more than every minute (approx).
3. **Accept any suitable answer:** Greenhouse; Oven; Traffic; People movement; Process control; Racing; Medical.
4. **Accept any two examples:** Thermal; Pressure; Light; Induction loops.

Page 67
1. A named data store on a backing storage device.
2. A group of letters after the file name that indicates the type of file.
3. An unstructured file.
4. **Accept any suitable answer:** You can't restore the original file; You may be able to detect the lower quality.

Page 69
1. A password that isn't easily guessed, e.g. a mixture of letters and numbers.
2. To allocate the right privileges.
3. Storing data that isn't in regular use.
4. To provide backup power and shut down properly if there's a power cut.

Page 71
1. A program, often harmful, that replicates itself.
2. Firewall.
3. A malicious program that's disguised as something you want / need.
4. Software or hardware that records or transmits every stroke made by a user.

Answers to Practice Questions
Pages 72–73
1. B
2. strong; hackers; numbers; ID; privileges
3. A
4. D, E, F
5. interface; computer; intuitive; mouse; icon
6. B, C, D
7. **a)** text **b)** input **c)** file **d)** archiving **e)** data
8. network; encrypted; packets; key; decrypt
9. C
10. change; absolute cell addressing; name; function
11. A2, B3, C5, D4, E1
12. Automated gives faster data entry, it's less likely to have mistakes and is cheaper because fewer humans are employed. **Do not accept an answer which simply says it's cheaper / faster.**

Modern Living

Quick Test Answers
Page 75
1. Internet Service Provider – it gives access to the Internet.
2. The Internet is the infrastructure (the linked networks). The World Wide Web is the collection of web sites. It's one of the services provided on the Internet.
3. Text with embedded links.
4. Through advertising.

Page 77
1. Don't meet them in private / alone; Don't give out your personal details.
2. To help choose employees; To check on the behaviour and character of staff.
3. A bogus letter, usually pretending to be from a bank, attempting to get bank details or passwords.
4. Using someone else's identity for personal gain.

Answers / Index

Modern Living (Cont.)

Page 79

1. **Accept any suitable example:** No queues; You can access your account at any time from anywhere; It's easy to keep in control.
2. Virtual Learning Environment – online resource for teaching and learning.
3. Human languages are unpredictable and translation is difficult to mechanise.
4. Up to date, can look worldwide.

Page 81

1. A web service where brief comments are posted.
2. Web mail can be accessed anywhere that the Internet can be accessed.
3. **Accept any suitable example:** Needs both people to be online at the same time; Needs broadband.
4. **Accept any suitable example:** Addictive; Privacy problems.

Page 83

1. Part of memory reserved for data being sent to or from the processor.
2. **Accept any suitable example:** Can see the view from the seat; Convenience; Easier to compare seats; Saves effort of travelling to the theatre; No queues.
3. High speed and quality displays are expected.
4. Watching buffered video as it's delivered.

Page 85

1. Hackers
2. **Accept two suitable examples:** Software; Music; Written material; Art
3. Unsolicited email
4. Finding evidence of crime in computer systems.

Page 87

1. The colours of the text and background can be changed.
2. Teach it to understand your voice.

3. A feature that lets you press a control key followed by a letter key instead of holding them down together.
4. Set the screen at the right height and use a comfortable chair.

Page 89

1. Arranging for alterations to be made visible in a document.
2. **Accept any suitable example:** No expense in arranging for storage security; No need to hire specialists in data storage.
3. The provision of software on a licensed basis online.
4. Loss of control over software and upgrades, and possibly data as well.

Page 91

1. Loading the operating system into memory.
2. Fragmentation of files, malware, running too many programs by default.
3. Can have personal preferences saved, privacy of work.
4. Protection against malware, speeds machine up, saves disk space.

Answers to Practice Questions

Pages 92–93

1. C
2. C
3. photos; privacy; friends; spam; phishing; identity theft
4. C, D, E
5. fragmentation; hard disk; defragmenter; utility; virus
6. A
7. **a)** Data Protection Act **b)** Cloud Computing **c)** blog **d)** buffer **e)** hypertext
8. braille; speech synthesiser; voice; sticky keys
9. There aren't any upgrade issues, it will always have the latest versions, there's no need to pay for data storage on site, there aren't any concerns about backing up, there's no need to employ own specialist staff.

Index